THE MYSTERY OF
GODLINESS

Books by W. Ian Thomas

The Saving Life of Christ
If I Perish, I Perish

W. IAN THOMAS

THE MYSTERY OF GODLINESS

Experiencing Christ in Us

CLC
PUBLICATIONS
Fort Washington, PA 19034

The Mystery of Godliness

Published by CLC Publications

U.S.A.
P.O. Box 1449, Fort Washington, PA 19034

UNITED KINGDOM
CLC International (UK)
51 The Dean, Alresford, Hampshire, SO24 9BJ

ISBN (paperback): 978-1-61958-186-9
ISBN (e-book): 978-1-61958-187-6

Printed in the United States of America

Dedicated to my wife,

JOAN,

and to my three sons,

CHRISTOPHER,

MARK

and

PETER,

for being such a wonderful

team in such a wonderful Savior.

Contents

1

The Quality of True Commitment

Jesus did not commit himself unto them, because he knew all men.
John 2:24 (KJV)

All that glitters is not gold, and in the light of all that we are about to consider, it may well be profitable for us to make a sober reevaluation of those standards of commitment that are prevalent in the church today and that pass muster for Christian dedication.

All too often quantity takes precedence over quality, and in this highly competitive age, those outward appearances of success that are calculated to enhance the reputation of the professional preacher or the prestige of those who have promoted him are of greater importance than the abiding consequences of his ministry.

In an unholy ambition to get results, the end too often justifies the means, with the result that the means are certainly not always beyond suspicion and the results, to say the least, extremely dubious!

In this unhappy situation both the pulpit and the pew carry their share of the blame, though I suspect that it starts in the pulpit. There are those who have insisted that to be valid, every spiritual transaction between the believer and his Lord must be matched by some outward physical act and that apart from the accompanying act, no worth can be attached to the inward spiritual transaction.

Inevitably on the basis of this unfounded supposition, the work of the Holy Spirit in any given meeting through the ministry of the preacher will be directly represented by the physical response of the congregation to some form of public appeal, invitation or so-called altar call—a term that is singularly inappropriate in view of the fact that the Lord Jesus Christ has "offered for all time a single sacrifice for sins" (Heb. 10:12). There is no place today for another sacrifice or another altar in the church of the redeemed. The altar has given place to a throne for the exalted Lamb!

The terrible dangers inherent in such a fallacy, however, are patently obvious.

The ambitious preacher, eager to climb the ladder of evangelical fame and not altogether unmoved by the plight of the lost and the needs of the saints, will be subject to a temptation so strong that for more than one it has proved to be irresistible: that of being heavily preoccupied with devising ways and means of ensuring that a large enough public response on the part of the congregation will adequately demonstrate the effectiveness of his preaching, vindicate his reputation, sufficiently reward the confidence of his sponsors and suitably impress the crowd. The preacher, of course, will not allow himself to be aware of the underlying motives that prompt the use of his clever techniques, being careful to persuade himself that they stem only from what he would describe as a genuine passion for souls. But the sorry spectacle is exposed for what it is by the apparent indifference on the part of the preacher to the tragic aftermath of his endeavors once the show is over!

It is little wonder that the pulpit, having drilled the pew into submission, now finds itself the victim of its own ill-conceived imposition, for the community that has been taught to accept outward, physical response to some public invitation as the criterion of spiritual success on the part of the preacher invariably demands this tangible evidence of success on every occasion in which he engages in his ministry.

Thus the pastor of a small church, trapped in the grip of this vicious circle, may succeed over a period of time in bringing the whole of his congregation down to the front to stand at the communion rail in response to his many appeals. But having had all his people down once, it will be incumbent upon him to get them down all over again and again and yet *again*—if his fervor and zeal are not to be called into question by his church officers and his pastorate, perhaps, be made vacant!

The pastor has no option under such circumstances but to whittle down the commitment he demands until its whole value and meaning has been lost; it can never be final, or he would preach himself out of business! Instead of being faced with complete capitulation to the Lord Jesus Christ and final, irrevocable abandonment to all His will, the believer is presented again and again with "baby" issues, all of which should be comprehended in the greater, basic issue of true discipleship.

It is much easier to confront a person with his sins than it is to confront him with his sin, for as will be fully demonstrated in later chapters of this book, sin is an attitude that affects a man's fundamental relationship to God. It has to do with what a man is, whereas sins have to do with what a man does—and we all have a happy knack of being able to detach what we do from what we are. We are all highly skilled in the art of self-justification and able to produce innumerable reasons as to why what we have done is excusable—even if it was wrong! We can even feel heroic, and almost virtuous, in accepting the blame for that which so obviously (to us!) was only the natural, almost inevitable, reaction to enticing, compelling or provocative circumstances or people. For this reason a man can admit and be sorry for what he has done without admitting that what he has done is a result of what he is.

On this basis a person may be called upon a hundred times to face the lesser issues of what he has done without once being confronted with the greater issue of what he is. Indeed, the "comfort" to be found in confession, bringing freedom from fear and relief to a bad conscience, will eliminate for him the need for any basic change in his fundamental relationship to God. This kind of confession falls hopelessly short of real repentance and remains unmatched by any change of purpose. Moses reduced his people to tears again and again—but it left them in the wilderness. They still had no heart for Canaan!

There was no lack of response to Moses' preaching, but the people of Israel would not do business with God. They said to Moses, "You speak to us, and we will listen; but do not let God speak to us, lest we die" (Exod. 20:19).

They wanted second-hand religion. They wanted neither godlessness nor godliness—they did not know how to live and were afraid to die. Commitment to them was on the installment system, and Moses was their broker!

Second-hand religion may keep a preacher in business and make him indispensable to his congregation, but it cannot produce discipleship. In it there will be no spontaneity of action nor any other evidence of that divine initiative in man that springs only from man's total availability to God.

True commitment to the Lord Jesus Christ gives the Lord right of way and releases His life through a believer in all the freshness and power of divine action so that, according to His gracious promise, out of his innermost being, "springs and rivers of living water" (John 7:38, AMP) may flow continuously. And no one has to push a river! It cuts its own channel and cleanses as it flows.

In drawing attention to those glaring abuses that have done so much to discredit modern evangelism and convention ministry, I do not suggest for one moment that there is not a legitimate place for the public confession of faith in Christ, nor would I insist that true commitment to Christ may never be accompanied by an outward witness to the fact. That would be to throw away the baby with the bathwater. Without a doubt there are many who have been greatly helped in their decision for Christ or in their commitment to Christ by a wise, gracious invitation to act rather than to delay further in yielding obedience to the truth.

My plea is simply for *reality*—on God's terms of reference! It is for this reason also that no matter how intensely I may dislike the shallowness and showmanship of many in their abuse of the holy art of preaching by the use of doubtful response techniques, I cannot, on the other hand, endorse in any way the empty accusation made by the champions of hollow, ritualistic formalism that all activity outside the established practice of religion within the "respectable" church systems is of necessity all mere ignorant emotionalism. That is sheer nonsense!

If there remains much to be desired in the quality of commitment prevalent today in evangelical circles and in the worldwide evangelistic outreach of that great body of born-again believers— the true church of Jesus Christ in all denominations—even more to be deplored are those wholesale opportunities for practicing hypocrisy provided by those formal, public acts of commitment to Christ common to so many of the denominations, which in the vast majority of cases are totally devoid of any spiritual content and serve only to satisfy the traditional niceties of religious observance in an otherwise godless society!

Whether it be by baptism as an infant or as an adult, by sprinkling or by immersion, whether it be by confirmation in the early teens or by any other public act of dedication and acceptance into full church membership, there must be very few in the Christianized countries of Western Europe who have not in one way or another "committed themselves to Christ." Yet by what strange twist of the mind or willful stretch of the imagination any ecclesiastical hierarchy of any given church system can credit this performance with any real spiritual validity, when over 90 percent of the populations of these countries never darken a church door to worship God, is beyond all intelligent explanation![1] The Lord Jesus Christ is neither accepted as Savior nor honored and obeyed as Lord, yet the rubber stamp of church approval has been granted. This is considered by the overwhelming majority to be an altogether adequate discharge of their responsibility toward

God and a formidable defense against the unwelcome attentions of those who would insist upon a reality of spiritual experience, which has neither been demanded nor expected by their "church!"

If church attendance in the United States, representing something like 60 percent of the population, far and away exceeds that of any other Western country at this time,[2] it should be a matter for genuine thankfulness to God. Yet there are few countries in the world where there are so many crimes of violence, so much juvenile delinquency, so much drug addiction and so many alcoholics and where there is such widespread graft and corruption in government and commerce. Are the ones responsible for this sorry record only those who have never conformed to the requirements of the church in some outward, formal act of dedication?

Why should international world Communism, with its fanatical convictions, its thorough indoctrination and utter dedication, be afraid of this flabby monster called the church, with its countless millions of nominal adherents who know neither conviction nor concern—who are colorless, spiritual non-entities knowing neither what they believe nor believing what they know! Such a church is utterly without any sense of mission and governed, by and large, by men who are themselves riddled through and through with infidelity, boastful of their own wanton repudiation of all the essential ingredients of the faith they profess to proclaim. It is a Christendom whose worst enemies are within its own ranks!

The word of God to the Jews in Paul's day might well be the word of God to Christendom today:

> As it is written, The name of God is maligned and blasphemed among the Gentiles because of you! [The words to this effect are from your own Scriptures.] . . . He is not a [real] Jew who is only one outwardly and publicly, nor is [true] circumcision something external and physical. But he is a Jew who is one inwardly, and [true] circumcision is of the heart, a spiritual and not a literal [matter]. His praise is not from men but from God. (Rom. 2:24, 28–29, AMP)

It was into just such a situation that the Lord Jesus Christ entered when at the Feast of the Passover He received such a tumultuous welcome in Jerusalem: "Hosanna to the Son of David!" the people cried. "Blessed is he who comes in the name of the Lord! Hosanna in the highest!" (Matt. 21:9).

No doubt the disciples were flushed with excitement and highly delighted that their Master should receive such a tremendous ovation—yet maybe there were some among them who had their misgivings. If only He could be prevailed upon not to say the wrong thing! If only they could persuade Him *just this once* not to do anything that would spoil it all!

But He did it again!

What a heartbreak Christ would be today to some well-meaning promotional committee or some business manager! It seemed that He always *did* the wrong thing or *said* the wrong thing just as He was on the crest of the wave and at the height of His popularity. He never seemed to understand what was in His own best interests!Amidst all this popular acclaim, the Lord Jesus Christ went straight to the temple.

> In the temple he found those who were selling oxen and sheep and pigeons, and the money-changers sitting there. And making a whip of cords, he drove them all out of the temple, with the sheep and oxen. And he poured out the coins of the money-changers and overturned their tables. And he told those who sold the pigeons, "Take these things away; do not make my Father's house a house of trade" (John 2:14–16).

Had He been prepared to accept "religion" as He found it and to recognize the status quo, no doubt the Lord Jesus Christ might well have found acceptance, even among the Pharisees. But He was a troublemaker. He dared to cleanse the temple!

Christ did not come to be accepted, nor was He looking for a job in contemporary religion. He came to cleanse the temple—and to do a bigger job than just to cleanse the temple in Jerusalem. He had come to cleanse the temples of men's hearts that they might be fit again to be "a dwelling place for God by the Spirit" (Eph. 2:22).

Challenged by the religious leaders to declare by what authority He presumed to disapprove and by what authority He was prepared to translate His disapproval into action, the Lord Jesus Christ gave this answer: "'Destroy this temple, and in three days I will raise it up.' . . . But he was speaking about the temple of his body" (John 2:19, 21).

Christ's death and resurrection were to be His mandate, and commitment to Christ for anything less than to be cleansed from sin and inhabited by God misses the whole point of the cross. The Lord will accept nothing less.

> When he was in Jerusalem at the Passover Feast, many believed in his name when they saw the signs that he was doing. But Jesus on his part did not entrust [commit] himself to them, because he knew all people and needed no one to bear witness about man, for he himself knew what was in man. (2:23–25)

Although the crowd appeared to have committed themselves to Christ, the quality of their commitment was such that He was not prepared to commit Himself to them!

What is the quality of *your* commitment to Christ?

You may be accepted into membership by the church, approved by your friends and entrusted with responsible office, but of what possible value can these things be if your commitment to Christ is such that He is not willing to commit Himself to you? The value of your commitment to Christ will only be the measure of *His* commitment to you!

The Lord Jesus Christ is the truth, and as in all other things "that pertain to life and godliness" (2 Pet. 1:3), He is the truth about true commitment. He was committed to the Father for all that to which the Father was committed in the Son, and He was supremely confident that the Father who dwelt in Him was gloriously adequate for all that to which He was committed. We know also that the Savior's commitment to His Father was such that the Father was completely committed to His Son!

The Lord Jesus Christ refused to be committed to the parochial needs of His own day and generation; He was not committed to the political situation in Palestine or to the emancipation of the Jewish nation from the Roman yoke! He was not committed to the pressing social problems of His time nor to one faction as opposed to another any more than today He is committed to the West against the East or to the Republicans against the Democrats (as though either were less wicked than the other!).

Christ was not even committed to the needs of a perishing world. He was neither unmindful nor unmoved by all these other issues, but as perfect man, He was committed to His Father and for that only to which His Father was committed in Him—exclusively!

> Jesus said to them, "When you have lifted up the Son of Man, then you will know that I am he, and that I do nothing on my own authority, but speak just as the Father taught me. And he who sent me is with me. He has not left me alone, for I always do the things that are pleasing to him." (John 8:28–29)

The Lord Jesus Christ was fully aware from the beginning of that to which the Father was committed in Him, for He was "the Lamb slain from the foundation of the world" (Rev. 13:8, KJV). Breaking the bread that pictured His body so soon to be broken and taking the wine as the symbol of His blood so soon to be shed, He could still look up into His Father's face and say thank You! He was completely committed, and so there were no other issues for Him to face.

The Lord Jesus Christ knew that before ever men like Wilberforce, Robert Moffat and David Livingstone could be committed to

Him for that to which He was to be committed in them—the abolition of slavery and the restoration of human dignity in the equality of all men under God—before ever men like Lord Shaftsbury, Dr. Barnardo and George Mueller could be committed to Him for that for which He was to be committed in them—to gather the ragged, half-starved orphans off the streets of Britain and restore hope to the unwanted—before He could attack the social evils and unschooled ignorance of a wanton nation through the persons of John Wesley and George Whitefield during the great evangelical awakening of their century or use Elizabeth Fry to bring about a reformation within an unpitying penal system that left a community of despair to languish, unloved and unmourned, in the vermin-ridden prisons of her land, then He the Son of God had first to commit Himself to the Father for that to which the Father was committed in Him!

The basis of His commitment to the Father is the basis upon which the Lord Jesus Christ claims your commitment to Him: that you are committed to Him for all that to which He is committed in you—*exclusively*!

You are not committed to a church or to a denomination or to an organization; as a missionary you are not committed to a mission board nor even to a mission field, and least of all are you committed to a need. You are committed to Christ for all that to which *Christ is committed in You*, and again I say—*exclusively*!

Thousands of earnest young Christians are challenged with the outworn slogan "The need is the call!" and are then immediately presented with a dozen different needs all representing a "call." When the invitation is given, hundreds stand in their confusion, swept to their feet on a wave of sentiment, yet it has been determined on a strictly statistical basis that out of every hundred who stand, not more than three will ever reach the mission field, and of those who do, almost 50 percent will return home to stay at home by the end of their first term overseas! Moses mistook the need for the call and, moved with compassion, went out to murder an Egyptian in defense of his brethren—and he became useless to God and man for forty years in the back side of the desert, herding a handful of sheep.

Abram committed himself to the will of God instead of to God whose will it was, and in his misguided zeal he tried to do God's work man's way. He felt that it was up to him and to Sarai to help God out of His predicament, for Sarai was old and had never borne children, for she was barren. So they had a committee meeting! After all, God had said that Abram was to have a son, and if this was God's will—and Abram was committed to God's will—then a son he must have at any price! It was a heavy price that Abram paid as Hagar, Sarai's maid, was summoned and ill-begotten Ishmael was born to become the father of the Arabs. The Jews in Israel today, surrounded by hostile Arab nations, reap the bitter harvest still of what was sown in Abraham's self-effort those many centuries before. Ishmael was the byproduct of a false commitment. Conceived in sincerity, he was the devil's *reasonable alternative* to faith!

When Isaac was born in God's perfect timing, fourteen years later, Ishmael mocked him—and he has been mocking him ever since. "Just as at that time he who was born according to the flesh persecuted him who was born according to the Spirit, so also it is now" (Gal. 4:29). "Oh that Ishmael might live before you!" (Gen. 17:18) is still the cry of those who in our own day and generation have yet to learn that "the son of the slave woman shall not inherit with the son of the free woman" (Gal. 4:30) and that there is *absolutely no substitute*, so far as God is concerned, for God's work done God's way!

When God tested Abraham and told him to offer up Isaac for a burnt offering, He said, "Take your son, your only son Isaac, whom you love, and go to the land of Moriah" (Gen. 22:2). Abraham might have argued with God and said, "But I have two sons! What about Ishmael? Isaac is not my *only* son!" God would have replied, "So far as I am concerned, only Isaac is your son. I do not recognize Ishmael—he should never have been born!"

The church of Jesus Christ today is plagued with Ishmaels clamoring to be recognized, but God will only honor Isaac—and Isaac's greater Son! Nothing infuriates the flesh more than failure to be recognized—and preaching that exposes the flesh for the wicked counterfeit it is must inevitably be the object of its venom and its wrath. "Too subjective!" "Unrealistic!" "Otherworldly!" "Oversimplified!" "Mere passivity!" "Pantheistic mysticism!"—these are some of the epithets with which Ishmael still mocks Isaac, with which the flesh resists the Spirit.

At God's command Abraham took Isaac, bound him, laid him on the altar he had built and took his knife to slay him, and with actions far more eloquent than words, he said to God by what he did, "You promised me Isaac! I did not see how You could do it, and in my unbelief and in my folly I produced my Ishmael; I committed myself to Your *will* and thought I was more competent than God. Now You tell me to slay him, my only son Isaac in whom You have promised that all the families of the earth shall be blessed. O God, if I slay him, I do not see *how* You can do it, but now I am committed to *You—exclusively*—and to all that for which You are committed in me. If slay him I *must*, then slay him I *will*—even if You have to raise him from the dead!" (see Heb. 11:17–19). And in so many words God said to Abraham, "Thank you, Abraham! That is all I wanted to know—now you can throw your knife away!"

> "Do not lay your hand on the boy or do anything to him, for now I know that you fear God. . . . By myself I have sworn, declares the LORD, because you have done this and have not withheld your son, your only son, I will surely bless you, and I will surely multiply your offspring as the stars of heaven and as the sand that is on the seashore. And your offspring shall possess the gate of his enemies, and in your offspring shall all the nations of the earth be blessed, because you have obeyed my voice." (Gen. 22:12, 16–18)

Abraham had learned the secret of true commitment, and he became "a friend of God" (James 2:23). This is *reality*—and this is discipleship! It is "godliness in action." Presenting all that you are—*nothing*—to all that He is—*everything*—you are committed to the Lord Jesus Christ *exclusively* for all that to which He is committed in you. And you may be supremely confident that He who dwells in *you* as the Father dwelt in *Him* is gloriously adequate for all that to which He is committed.

Are you prepared for this to be the quality of your commitment to Christ? If so, then every lesser issue has been comprehended in the greater. It is now no longer necessary for me to ask you whether you are prepared to go to the mission field! It is now no longer necessary for me to ask you whether you are prepared to put your bank account at Christ's disposal, or your time or your home, or to face you with any other issue I could think of! You would say to me at once, "These issues now have all been settled—finally, once and for all! If Christ is committed in me to go to the mission field, I am already committed to Him for this! If He is committed in me to use the very last dollar I possess and every other dollar I shall ever earn, I am already committed to Him for this and for everything and anything else to which He may be committed in me! There are no more issues for me to face—*only His instructions to obey!* I know too that *for all His will*, I have *all that He is*—and this is *all* I need to know!"

Indeed it is—for you cannot have *more!*

And you need never have *less!*

2

How to Do the Impossible

He answered them, "You give them something to eat."
Mark 6:37

"It is not difficult for man to live the Christian life," some-body once said. *"It is a sheer impossibility!"*

A sheer impossibility, that is, without Christ—but for *all that He says,* you have *all that He is,* and that is *all that it takes!*

As we have already seen, this was the lesson that Abra-ham learned—he was "fully convinced that God was able to do what he had promised" (Rom. 4:21)—and Mary too, as we shall see later: "The angel answered her . . . 'Nothing will be impossible with God.' And Mary said, 'Behold, I am the servant of the Lord; let it be to me according to your word'" (Luke 1:35–38).

It was this same lesson that the Lord Jesus Christ wished to teach His disciples, but they were very slow to learn—and so are we!

"He saw a great crowd, and he had compassion on them, because they were like sheep without a shepherd. And he began to teach them many things" (Mark 6:34). Luther's translation of this verse has always been a source of great comfort to me as a teacher—"He preached a long sermon." And it was a long sermon! It lasted right on into the evening, so much so that the disciples began to get quite worried as to what they were going to do with this great crowd of people! "This is a desolate place," they said to the Master. "Send them away to ... buy themselves something to eat" (Mark 6:35–36).

To the disciples this seemed the only reasonable, sensible thing to do in the face of a situation that threatened to become increasingly embarrassing. There were five thousand men, Matthew records, "beside women and children" (Matt. 14:21), and if meetings in those days were anything like meetings in these days, five thousand men *plus* women and children was a big meeting! The crowd was tired, hot and hungry, and with no prospect of feeding them, there appeared to the disciples no alternative but to remind the Lord Jesus Christ of the lateness of the hour and to say to Him in so many words, "Master, we simply *must* get these people off our hands!"

There is always a *reasonable* alternative to faith!

The Lord Jesus Christ answered them and said, "You give them something to eat"—in other words, "You don't send hungry people away—you feed them!"

"Shall we go and buy two hundred denarii worth of bread and give it to them to eat?" (Mark 6:37), asked the bewildered disciples. "Master, that's a sheer impossibility!"

"Exactly! To you it is a sheer impossibility," the Lord Jesus Christ might well have replied, "and that is why we are going to do it. I am going to show you how to do the impossible!"

The Christian life can only be explained in terms of Jesus Christ. If your life as a Christian can still be explained in terms of *you*—*your* personality, *your* willpower, *your* gift, *your* talent, *your* money, *your* courage, *your* scholarship, *your* dedication, *your* sacrifice or *your* anything—then although you may *have* the Christian life, you are not yet *living* it!

If the way you live your life as a Christian can be explained in terms of you, what have you to offer to the man who lives next door? The way he lives his life can be explained in terms of him, and so far as he is concerned, you happen to be "religious"—but he is not. Christianity may be your hobby, but it is not his, and there is nothing about the way you practice it that strikes him as at all remarkable. There is nothing about you that leaves him guessing and nothing commendable about you of which he does not feel himself equally capable— without the inconvenience of his becoming a Christian!

It is only when your quality of life *baffles* the neighbors that you are likely to *impress* them! It has got to become patently obvious to others that the kind of life you are living is not only *highly commendable* but that it is beyond all *human explanation*—that it is beyond the consequences of man's capacity to *imitate* and, however little they may understand this, clearly the consequence only of God's capacity to *reproduce Himself* in you.

In a nutshell, this means that your fellowmen must become convinced that the Lord Jesus Christ of whom you speak is essentially Himself the ingredient of the life you live!

How did Christ feed the five thousand? To discover this we need to turn to the record found in the sixth chapter of John's Gospel, for here it is as though the apostle takes a magnifying glass and allows us to examine the story in greater detail.

"Lifting up his eyes, then, and seeing that a large crowd was coming toward him, Jesus said to Philip, 'Where are we to buy bread, so that these people may eat?' He said this to test him, for he himself knew what he would do" (John 6:5–6). Was Christ seeking advice when He asked Philip this question? Was He at a loss to know what to do? Most certainly not, for "he himself knew what he would do." He knew *exactly* what He would do! He always does, no matter with what situation He may be confronted at any time and anywhere. Nothing ever takes Him by surprise, and nothing shocks Him. He is *never* baffled—*never* bewildered! He is the God who declares "the end from the beginning" and upon whose head no emergency can ever break. As I once heard a noted Christian psychologist, Dr. Cramer, remark, "The Lord Jesus Christ was completely 'panic-proof'"—and He still is!

Are you?

This will be singularly characteristic of you if you are really enjoying the life of the Lord Jesus Christ. You too will be "panic-proof"! Yours will be "the peace of God, which surpasses all understanding" (Phil. 4:7)—that is to say, peace that in the light of all the circumstances is beyond all human explanation!

Christ was not seeking advice when He asked Philip this question, nor was He trying to discover anything about Philip, for again and again occasions are recorded in the Gospels in which the Lord Jesus Christ replied to a person's *thoughts*.

He knew everything there was to know about Philip's heart and a whole lot more than Philip knew himself, as He knows everything there is to know about your heart and mine! "Not a creature exists that is concealed from His sight, but all things are open and exposed, naked and defenseless to the eyes of Him with Whom we have to do" (Heb. 4:13, AMP). Then why did Christ ask this question?

He asked the question because He wanted Philip to dis-cover something about himself. He wanted him to discover the utter poverty of his experience of Christ—how very far short he fell of living miraculously! Nor was it for Philip alone to make this discovery, but for all the Lord's disciples.

"Philip answered him, 'Two hundred denarii worth of bread would not be enough for each of them to get a little'" (John 6:7). With what then was Philip reckoning? Was it with the presence and power of the Lord Jesus Christ? No! Just with the money in the bag! Beyond that for him, in this situation, there was no further horizon. So far as Philip was concerned, for all the difference that the presence of Christ made to the problem, the Lord might just as well have been dead!

Had a materialistically minded atheist been consulted in the face of this dilemma, the first question he would have asked is, "How much money do you have?" What then would have been the difference between Philip's outlook and that of an unbelieving atheist? There would have been no difference!

Philip had not learned to *reckon* with Christ!

Because to Philip their financial resources were all-impor-tant, Jesus Christ was unimportant. There was nothing about the kind of life Philip was living as an apostle that could not have been given a dollar equivalent!

What are *you* reckoning with? Are you *really* reckoning with Christ? Upon what basis have you evaluated the many different situations that have arisen within the last twenty-four hours before taking this book in your hand and read-ing these pages? Did you take the Lord Jesus Christ into ac-count—or did you consider Him to be irrelevant?

Remember that it is precisely those areas of your life in which you have not considered Christ to be relevant in which as yet you have not repented. In these areas you are still trying to be adequate without Him—trying to be the cause of your own effect. And if *you* are the cause, there will certainly be nothing miraculous about the effect!

In your disillusionment you may well try, as the disciples did, to get the situation off your hands, convinced that you are as inadequate with Christ as without Him! Then you *will* be miserable! Better not visit the neighbors *that* day!

The Lord Jesus Christ said, "How many loaves do you have? Go and see" (Mark 6:38). And when they went, they found Andrew arguing with a small boy. I can imagine that the conversation ran something like this: "It's kind of you, laddie, and I will tell the Master that you offered, but I don't think we should disturb Him now. You see, He's busy—and in any case, five loaves and two fish just aren't enough to go around! That lunch is just about your size—you could wrap yourself around that! But thanks again, lad—thanks a lot! I'll tell the Master, I promise!"

Indignantly the boy replied, "I don't care whether I've got *five* loaves or *fifty* loaves or *five hundred* loaves or *five thousand* loaves—*that* does not matter! *Please take me to that man!* That is *all* that matters!"

At that moment the others arrived on the scene, and maybe if the Master had not sent them, Andrew never would have brought that boy to the Lord Jesus. Even when he did, it was only to apologize! "One of his disciples, Andrew, Simon Peter's brother, said to him, 'There is a boy here who has five barley loaves and two fish, but what are they for so many?'" (John 6:8–9).

Andrew, I am sure, was not unkind to the boy. I believe from the record that we have of him in the Gospels that Andrew was of a particularly kindly disposition, and maybe that was why the lad felt at liberty to speak to him—perhaps a friendly smile had given him the invitation! Andrew, I believe, had a face like a doormat—one that has "Welcome" woven into it!

Some folk wonder why it is that no one ever comes to them for counsel—they have faces like a notice on the gate: "Beware of the Dog!"

Be that as it may, and kind as he may have been, what was Andrew reckoning with? Was he reckoning with the presence and the power of Christ? No! Just with five barley loaves and two small fish. And because these to him were all-important, Jesus Christ was unimportant!

On the other hand, because to this small boy the Lord Jesus Christ was *all-important*, the vastness of the need and the poverty of supply were totally *unimportant*. The lad had already learned the secret of living miraculously, for he had learned in his own way to *reckon with Christ!*

This is always a precious story to me, for the Lord Jesus Himself "knew what he would do" long before Andrew spoke to that small boy or ever anyone else had recognized the potential in him. Christ knew his heart and had already chosen him!

In *every* crowd there is always *one* at least whose heart He knows and whom He has already chosen. To *discern* that one and to bring that one—without apology—is the holy art of soul-winning. "Whoever captures souls is wise" (Prov. 11:30). It will not always be the most prominent nor even the most promising person—maybe just a lad with a lunch bag and a twinkle in his eye!

"Jesus then took the loaves, and when he had given thanks, he distributed them to those who were seated. So also the fish, as much as they wanted" (John 6:11). Whatever second thoughts some "learned theologians" may have had about the memorable events that took place on that exciting day, those who were present and were witnesses were obviously in no doubt at all as to what had really happened, for "when the people saw the sign that he had done, they said, 'This is indeed the Prophet who is to come into the world!'" (6:14). They recognized the fact at once, as they watched the Lord Jesus Christ at work, that here was a man for whose activities there could be absolutely no explanation at all apart from God!

There are those, of course, who would have you accept "the little paper bag" theory. They would seek to persuade you that when the crowd saw the unselfishness of the little boy, as he took out his lunch pack and was willing to share his five loaves and two small fish with the multitude, they were so touched and ashamed that suddenly about five thousand "little paper bags" appeared—and everyone began to share with everyone else what until then they had been hiding underneath their shirts!

Isn't that sweet? Some folks call this scholarship and grant doctorates on the strength of it! The twelve baskets might have been better used to gather up the litter than to gather up the fragments that remained!

If you only have a little paper-bag god, then you must content yourself with little paper-bag miracles—but with *our God* "nothing will be impossible" (Luke 1:37)!

> When they had eaten their fill, he told his disciples, "Gather up the leftover fragments, that nothing may be

lost." So they gathered them up and filled twelve baskets *with fragments from the five barley loaves* left by those who had eaten. (John 6:12–13)

There was a secret to the miracle that the Lord Jesus Christ performed—a secret that He wanted to share with His disciples and that He wants to share with you too. To miss this is to miss the object of the exercise, the lesson to be learned! It is at the very heart of the mystery of godliness: it is written that "Jesus then took the loaves, and *when he had given thanks*, he distributed them to those who were seated." Whom did Christ thank? Did He thank Himself? God as God certainly has no one to thank but Himself, and Jesus Christ was God! It is quite obvious that the Lord Jesus Christ as the Son gave thanks to His Father as God, and in His perfect role as the perfect man, He relentlessly refused to be the cause of His own effect!

As the Creator God, there is absolutely no doubt but that Christ could Himself have fed the five thousand—or, for that matter, five hundred times five thousand. But then He would not have been behaving as man, He would have been behaving as God. And as we shall discover later, had He both *been* and *behaved* as God, no one would have seen Him! No one has ever seen God at any time (see 1:18)!

As the "only begotten Son," Christ "declared" the Father (1:18, KJV) in all that He said, in all that He did and in all that He was. And, as I shall remind you yet again, the Lord Jesus said, "The Father who dwells in me does his works" (14:10).

So who fed the five thousand? The Father through the Son!

In spite of His eternal equality with the Father and with the Holy Spirit in the Trinity of the Deity, the Lord Jesus

Christ for our sakes "made Himself *nothing*" (Phil. 2:7, NIV) that the Father might be everything and be glorified in Him! In an attitude of total dependence, He exercised toward the Father as God that perfect faith-love relationship for which man, by Christ Himself, had been created!

Confronted by this hungry multitude of people, Christ deliberately subjected Himself to the limitations that He as the creative Word had imposed upon man as His own creation. He exposed the situation to His Father, and in humble dependence upon His adequacy, said quite simply, "Thank You"—and then He reckoned with the Father as He divided the loaves and the fishes.

That is how to do the impossible!

When the Lord Jesus Christ raised Lazarus from the dead, how did He do it?

"Take away the stone," He said to Martha, the sister of him that was dead, but she said to Him, "Lord, by this time there will be an odor, for he has been dead four days" (John 11:39). Clearly by any natural standards the situation was impossible, yet Christ said to Martha, "Did I not tell you that if you believed you would see the glory of God?" (11:40). Once more the Father was to be glorified in and through the Son! "So they took away the stone" (11:41) from the place where the dead was laid.

Christ on this occasion was confronted by a man four days dead and with all the indisputable evidences of decay as He stood before the open cave. Was this to be His problem? Was His the right to challenge the awful finality of death? The *power* indeed He had, for He was God, but not the *right*, for He was man! "For Christ did not please himself" (Rom. 15:3). How then did Christ do the impossible and raise this man from the dead?

Christ raised Lazarus from the dead just as He had fed the five thousand. He exposed the situation to His Father, and in humble dependence upon His adequacy He said quite simply, "Thank You." Then He reckoned with the Father as He cried with a loud voice, "'Lazarus, come out.' The man who had died came out" (John 11:43–44).

It was just as simple as that! "Jesus lifted up his eyes and said, 'Father, I thank you that you have heard me. I knew that you always hear me, but I said this on account of the people standing around, that they may believe that you sent me'" (11:41–42).

Christ sought then, as He had sought by the feeding of the five thousand, to demonstrate the principle by which He lived His supernatural life as man on earth: that all men might believe that He was the sent One and His Father the Sender and that they might know and believe that as the *Father* sent *Him*, so *He* sends *them*—to live miraculously!

"Truly, truly, I say to you, whoever believes in me will also do the works that I do; and greater works than these will he do, because I am going to the Father" (14:12). The Lord Jesus Christ wants to be to you now all that the Father was to Him then—God—if only you will be to Him now all that He was to the Father then—man!

Have you learned to expose *every* situation to the Lord Jesus Christ in humble dependence upon His adequacy, then simply to say "Thank You" and to reckon with Him as you act to meet that situation?

By the feeding of the five thousand in humble dependence on the Father, the Lord Jesus Christ showed His disciples how to do the impossible and live miraculously!

How much did His disciples learn? *Nothing!*

3

I AM—You Are!

They did not understand about the loaves,
but their hearts were hardened.
Mark 6:52

Get them off our hands! Send them away, for they have nothing to eat!" That was the pitiful cry of the disciples as they came in panic to the Lord Jesus Christ. But instead He *fed* the hungry multitude *and got His disciples off His hands!*

One of the hardest lessons for us to learn is that none of us is ever indispensable to God. But God is always indispensable to us! "Those who ate the loaves were five thousand men. Immediately [Jesus] made his disciples get into the boat and go before him to the other side, to Bethsaida, while he dismissed the crowd" (Mark 6:44–45).

Why did He send His disciples away? He sent them away because they had learned *nothing*—absolutely *nothing!* "They failed to consider or understand [the teaching and meaning of the miracle of] the loaves; [in fact] their hearts had grown callous [had become dull and had lost the power of understanding]" (6:52, AMP). Their hearts were hardened!

Called to be apostles and the closest companions of the Savior during His earthly ministry, they lived and worked and walked and talked with Him. They shared His platform, basked in His limelight and had a name for being His most devoted followers. Yes, they were *big names*—but they were *big names* with *hard hearts!*

To hold office does not in itself make a man spiritual. Unfortunately, all too often it is the *unspiritual* who fight and edge their way into office, where the flesh can indulge its insatiable appetite for position and power. For the flesh loves to be recognized, consulted, honored, admired and obeyed!

You may be a bishop, a pastor, the church secretary, an elder or a deacon; you may be the president, principal or dean of a college; you may be chairman of some mission board or the field director as the senior missionary on the field; you may hold any office of any kind, however distinguished it may be—*and still have a hard heart.* Where this is the case and where there is real business to be done, you must not be surprised if Christ gets you off His hands too—unless and until you repent.

> God is not impressed with the positions that men hold and He is not partial and recognizes no external distinctions. (Gal. 2:6, AMP)

> You say, I am rich, I have prospered, and I need nothing, not realizing that you are wretched, pitiable, poor, blind, and naked. . . . Those whom I love, I reprove and discipline, so be zealous and repent. (Rev. 3:17, 19)

Do not allow the poverty of self-sufficiency to rob you of the miraculous. It is a particularly subtle form of conceit that denies to God the possibility of doing what we consider to be beyond the bounds of our own carnal self-esteem.

How patient Christ was with His disciples!

Having learned nothing, they were given the same lesson all over again, but in another setting. A setting, indeed, that was little to the liking of the disciples themselves, for having been sent away, they found themselves "a long way from the land, beaten by the waves, for the wind was against them" (Matt. 14:24).

With their backs bent to the oars, perspiration pouring down their faces and every muscle aching, they battled against the storm. Darkness had already fallen, and the shoreline had long been lost to sight. As the mountainous waves beat into the little boat, threatening to swamp it and send it to the bottom, the disciples began to wonder whether they would ever reach their destination. But "in the fourth watch of the night [Jesus] came to them"—doing what? *Doing the impossible*—"walking on the sea" (14:25)!

How did the Lord Jesus Christ do the impossible? How did He walk on the water? He did this as He had fed the five thousand and as He had raised Lazarus from the dead. He *reckoned* with His Father—just one step at a time—and for every step He took He said, "Thank You, Father!"

Christ demonstrated to His disciples that everything that threatened to be *over their heads*, His Father had already put *under His feet!* What is it that is threatening *you*? What makes you afraid? What is it from which you are running away? Is there something that seems about to swamp your little boat—that baffles, beats and bewilders you? Here is good news for you: there is nothing that could ever threaten to be over your head that He does not already have under His feet—and He is waiting for you to share His victory! "When the disciples saw Him walking on the sea, they were terrified and said, It is a ghost! And they screamed out with fright. But instantly He spoke to them, saying, Take courage! I AM; stop being afraid!" (Matt. 14:26–27, AMP).

They thought they had seen a ghost! A man walking on the water—that is impossible! But the Lord Jesus said, "I AM: stop being afraid!" In so many words, Christ said to His disciples, "I AM—all that you could ever need at *any* time, in *any* storm—and all that I AM you *have*! Stop being frightened!"

"Peter answered him, 'Lord, if it is you, command me to come to you on the water'" (14:28). "Master," Peter might have said, "if it be *You*, then please put under *my* feet what is already under *Your* feet!" We can almost imagine the smile that must have been on the face of the Master. "Why, Peter! That is all I have been waiting for! I have simply been waiting for *you* to reckon with Me as *I* reckon with My Father! Come on! Come!"

At the command of the Lord Jesus Christ, Peter stepped over the side, and when "Peter got out of the boat," what do you think he did? He did the *impossible*—he "walked on the water and came to Jesus" (14:29).

One step at a time, and for every step he took, you could almost have heard Peter crying in his excitement, "This is wonderful, Lord! Thank You! Thank You, Lord! This is tremendous. This is an entirely new experience for me—I have never walked on water before! Thank You, Lord! Thank You!"

As Peter kept his eyes upon the Savior and related his situation to Christ for every step he took, he shared the victory of his Lord. The impossible became possible!

Suddenly an unkind wave slapped Peter on the face from one side, and yet another hit him from the other side, and he almost lost his balance! His attention was distracted from

Christ, and once more he became aware of the howling of the wind and the swelling of the waters. He stopped relating the situation *to the Lord* and began again to relate the situation to *himself*, and he began immediately to think, *I can't do this! A man can't walk on water—that's impossible!* And he was quite right! Peter began to go down for a ducking, and "he cried out, 'Lord, save me'" (Matt. 14:30).

The Lord Jesus Christ immediately stretched forth His hand and caught him. He recaptured Peter's attention and once more put the threatening waters beneath the disciple's feet, and they walked *together* until they were come into the ship, and "the wind ceased" (14:32). The exercise was over!

What do you think Christ said to Peter? Perhaps you think He should have congratulated him! "Peter, I just want you to know how immensely I appreciated your *tremendous faith!* The way you got out of that boat and walked toward Me was a masterpiece! I *must* congratulate you—I haven't seen such a great faith in a long time!" Is that what Christ said? Oh, no! Far from it! Instead He said to him, "O you of little faith, why did you doubt?" (14:31). In so many words He said, "It is not *difficult*, Peter, to do the impossible! It is *inevitable* so long as you reckon with Me! Why did you stop reckoning? I can't *congratulate* you, Peter. I'm just sorry that your faith was so small!"

The lesson, however, was not in vain. "Those in the boat worshiped him, saying, 'Truly you are the Son of God'" (14:33).

In the midst of the storm, when everything was against them, the Lord Jesus Christ appeared and said, "*I AM*; stop being afraid," and now at last they had learned to say, "Truly *you are* the Son of God." If there is nothing else that you remember of all that has been written in this book, this in itself would comprehend the whole relationship of God to man and man to God: "Whoever would draw near to God must believe that he exists"—"You are"—"and that he rewards those who seek him"—"I AM"! (Heb. 11:6). All that you could ever need at any time, in *any* storm, "and all that I AM," He says, "you *have!*"

It may be that your need is still that of a sinner seeking forgiveness; you need to be redeemed, and you are still trying to find your way back to God and godliness. Christ is saying to you now, as He said to His disciples of old in the Upper Room after He was risen from the dead, "See my hands and my feet, that it is I myself" (Luke 24:39). In other words, "I AM—all that a guilty sinner needs! The wounds in My hands and My feet are the hallmarks of My Saviorhood; put your trust in Me, and I will save you!"

All you need to say to Him is this: "Lord Jesus, *You are!* For *me*—just what I need! *My* Savior and *my* Redeemer—forever!"

> Behold Him there, the risen Lamb!
> My perfect, spotless righteousness,
> The great unchangeable I AM,
> The King of glory and of grace.

You will be redeemed, and He will give you *life.* By the gift of His indwelling Holy Spirit, Jesus Christ will give you *His* life, and this is what it means to "*live* by the Spirit." But "if we live by the Spirit, let us also keep in step with the Spirit" (Gal. 5:25). And *this* is what it means to "*keep in step with* the Spirit": to take one step at a time, and for every new situation into which every new step takes you, no matter what it may be, to hear Christ saying to your heart, "I AM!" and then to look up into His face by faith and say, "*You are! That is all I need to know, Lord, and I thank You, for You are never *less* than adequate!"

Thus to walk is to experience with Paul the apostle,

> I know how to be abased and live humbly in straitened
> circumstances, and I know also how to enjoy plenty
> and live in abundance. I have learned in any and all
> circumstances the secret of facing every situation,
> whether well-fed or going hungry, having a sufficiency
> and enough to spare or going without and being in want.
> I have strength for all things in Christ Who empowers
> me [I am ready for anything and equal to anything
> through Him Who infuses inner strength into me; I am
> self-sufficient in Christ's sufficiency]. (Phil. 4:12–13, AMP)

Without this kind of faith it is impossible to please God, for without this kind of faith, it is impossible for God to reproduce His character in you—and that is godliness!

True godliness leaves the world convinced beyond a shadow of a doubt that the only explanation for *you* is *Jesus Christ*—to whose eternally unchanging and altogether adequate "I AM!" your heart has learned to say with unshatterable faith, *"You are!"*

That is really all you need to know! "All of us, as with unveiled face, [because we] continued to behold [in the Word of God] as in a mirror the glory of the Lord, are constantly being transformed into His very own image in ever increasing splendor and from one degree of glory to another; [for this comes] from the Lord [Who is] the Spirit" (2 Cor. 3:18, AMP).

4

The Nature of the Mystery

Great indeed, we confess, is the mystery of godliness:
[God] was manifested in the flesh.
1 Timothy 3:16

G odliness is a mystery! Fail to grasp this fact, and you will never understand the nature of godliness.

God did not create you to have just an ape-like capacity to imitate God. There would be no mystery in that, nor would this lift you morally much above the status of a monkey or a parrot! The capacity to imitate is vested in the one who imitates and does not derive from nor necessarily share the motives of the person being imitated, who remains passive and impersonal to the act of imitation.

The kindness and sheer generosity of a certain individual may be an act of pure benevolence, a genuine, selfless expression of the love of God. You may be tempted to imitate this person's act, to reproduce it in kind or even to outmatch it, but *your motives may be entirely evil* though the act identical!

Pride may persuade you not to be outdone. Jealousy may compel you to prove that the other party is not "the only pebble on the beach." You may resent the gratitude or affection or respect that the other person, however unintentionally, has justly earned and deserved, or you may feel that the regard in which the other is now held may lessen your own influence over the future course of events!

In this case, you may deceive the undiscerning with your generosity and achieve your ends, but your "generosity" will not be godliness—your "generosity" will be *sin!*

In direct contrast to this, godliness—or Godlikeness—is the direct and exclusive consequence of God's activity in man. Not the consequence of your capacity to imitate God but the consequence of God's capacity to *reproduce Himself* in you! This is the nature of the mystery of godliness! Remove the mystery or try to explain it away, and the result must inevitably be disastrous, for you will no longer be anchored to anything absolute. You will be at liberty to choose your own god—the object of your own imitation—and your "godliness" will be the measure of your conformity to the object of your choice.

This, in point of fact, is what has been happening all through human history since Adam repudiated the basic principles of his own humanity and decided to go it alone—without God. Man may hide from God—as Adam did—but still the voice of God pursues him, echoing within the spiritual vacuum of his homesick, godless soul with all the relentless persistency of a love that never fails, crying, "Son of Adam, where *are you?* Where *are you?* Where *are you?*"

This is what makes even the most degenerate individual incurably religious, even though his religion may be most horrible in character and may assume the most hideous of forms. Sometimes it even disguises itself as a political creed, as in the national socialism of Adolf Hitler or the atheistic communism of Karl Marx, which for all their political flavor and advertised contempt for religion *are nonetheless religions in themselves.* It is one of the subtleties of Satan that causes men to flee from God and seek to silence *His voice in the very practice of religion.*

So it is that man, to suit his own convenience, has reduced God to a theological formula, an ethical code or political program, a theatrical performance in a religious setting, the hero worship of some vivid personality of noble (or doubtful) reputation or some dreamed-up image of his own better self. Everything from a white cow to the wind in the trees—or a Christless "Christianity"—has been and still remains the object of man's idolatry!

The moment you come to realize that only *God* can make a man godly, you are left with no option but to *find* God and to *know* God and to let God *be* God in you and through you, whoever He may be. This will leave you with no margin for picking and choosing—for there is only *one* God, and He is absolute, and He made you expressly for *Himself!*

Beware lest even as a Christian, you fall into Satan's trap! You may have *found* and come to *know* God in the Lord Jesus Christ, receiving Him sincerely as your Redeemer, yet if you do not enter into the mystery of godliness and allow God to *be* in you the origin of His own image, you will seek to be godly by submitting yourself to external rules and regulations and by conformity to behavior patterns imposed upon you by the particular Christian society that you have chosen and in which you hope to be found acceptable.

You will in this way perpetuate the pagan habit of practicing religion in the energy of the flesh, and in the very pursuit of righteousness you will commit idolatry in honoring Christianity more than Christ!

> If then you have died with Christ to material ways of look-
> ing at things and have escaped from the world's crude and
> elemental notions and teachings of externalism, why do
> you live as if you still belong to the world? [Why do you
> submit to rules and regulations?—such as] Do not handle
> [this], Do not taste [that], Do not even touch [them], Re-
> ferring to things all of which perish with being used. To
> do this is to follow human precepts and doctrines. Such
> [practices] have indeed the outward appearance [that
> popularly passes] for wisdom, in promoting self-imposed
> rigor of devotion and delight in self-humiliation and se-
> verity of discipline of the body, but they are of no value in
> checking the indulgence of the flesh (the lower nature).
> [Instead, they do not honor God but serve only to indulge
> the flesh.] (Col. 2:20–23, AMP)

One Aspect of the Mystery: God Cannot Be Seen

"God said, 'Let us make man in our image, after our likeness' . . . So God created man in his own image, in the image of
God he created him" (Gen. 1:26–27). This does not mean that
man was created physically in the shape of God nor that God
looks like a man.

We do not know what God looks like, for "no one has
ever seen God" (John 1:18). The Bible declares expressly that
God is *invisible*:

> To the King of the ages, immortal, invisible, the only
> God, be honor and glory forever and ever. . . . [He] alone
> has immortality, who dwells in unapproachable light,
> whom no one has ever seen or can see. To him be honor
> and eternal dominion. Amen. (1 Tim. 1:17; 6:16)

The Bible is equally emphatic concerning the absolute deity of the Son and His equality with the Father, which the

Lord Jesus Christ never once repudiated, yet no man has seen God at any time. But did no one ever see Jesus Christ? This is part of the mystery! "He was manifested in the flesh" (1 Tim. 3:16), and further, "the only God, who is at the Father's side, he has made him known" (John 1:18).

Philip said, "Lord, show us the Father, and it is enough for us." And the Lord Jesus replied, "Have I been with you so long, and you still do not know me, Philip? Whoever has seen me has seen the Father. How can you say, 'Show us the Father?'" (14:8–9). To reconcile this statement of the Lord Jesus and the fact of His own deity with the fact that no man has seen God at any time would seem at first to present an insuperable problem, for we are presented with the baffling conclusion that in spite of His total equality within the Trinity of Deity, it was possible, nineteen hundred years ago, for men on earth to look into the face of the Son, see the Father and yet not see God!

The solution to this mystery, as I trust you will discover, is really remarkably simple—for in Jesus Christ Himself it has become an open secret and one that He invites you to share with Him!

It is of paramount importance from the very outset that we recognize the fact that when the Lord Jesus Christ was here on earth, He could *be* God and *be* man at one and the same time, but He could not *behave* as God and *behave* as man at one and the same time.

Allow me to explain a little, for to understand this is calculated to bring you untold comfort and encouragement and to give you an entirely new concept of the Christian life and a richer, fuller experience of Christ Himself.

Man was created in such a way that he could bear the image of God without God Himself becoming *visible* so that not man's *physical form* but his *capacity to behave* was designed to be the means through which God intended to express His nature and His character. As we have already seen, however, this godliness, or Godlikeness, was not to have been an imitation of God by man but the direct result of the activity of God in man. In other words—God Himself behaving in and through you!

Man's behavior as the *effect* was to have been the result of God's behavior as the *cause*. The former was to have been the "brightness," or the out-shining, of the latter's glory, the "express *image*" of His person (Heb. 1:3, KJV). The image was to have been *visible*, while God's person still remained *invisible*!

Had the Lord Jesus Christ been the source of His own godliness, as He could have been, He would have been *behaving* as God only—both *cause* and *effect*. And He had the right to behave as God only—for He was and is God. But He could not then have behaved as man. He would not in point of fact have been godly, or Godlike—He would just simply have been God. But "no one has ever seen God" (John 1:18), so had He in this world both *been* and *behaved* as God, no one would have been able to see Him! In order to be seen, He had to be made "in the likeness of men" and be found "in human form" (Phil. 2:7–8) and to *behave* as man.

To perform in perfection on earth the role for which Christ, as God, had created man, He had of His own free volition to accept the limitations imposed upon mankind and to allow the Father, *as God*, to be the origin of all His own behavior *as man*. In this way His godliness as man was derived directly and exclusively from the activity of the Father in and through the Son.

In His sinless and perfect humanity, Christ became "the sole expression of the glory of God [the Light-being, the out-raying or radiance of the divine], and He is the perfect imprint and very image of [God's] nature" (Heb. 1:3, AMP). Or, as Paul declares, "He is the exact likeness of the unseen God [the visible representation of the invisible]" (Col. 1:15, AMP). This will help us to understand more fully what the Bible means when it says, "He humbled himself by becoming obedient" (Phil. 2:8). This does not mean simply that He accepted the physical limitations of the human body but that He adopted an attitude of total dependence upon the Father. He denied Himself the right to exercise all those prerogatives of deity that were undoubtedly His by virtue of the fact that He was both God and man at one and the same time. Christ deliberately made Himself of "no reputation" (2:7, KJV) and consistently refused to be the cause of His own effect, declaring emphatically, "I can do nothing on my own" (John 5:30).

To use a simple illustration, no man has seen electricity at any time, yet an electric light bulb is so designed that whenever it receives the invisible electric current, expression is given to the *invisible* in terms of *light*.

It would not be true to say that the *bulb* is giving light, for it has no power to do so apart from the current that it receives—its behavior as a light-giver is the direct and exclusive consequence of the activity of the electricity in it and through it. The current is the *cause*, light is the *effect*—and though one can see the effect, he still cannot see the cause, though both represent the same source of energy!

A man can enjoy the light, but he still cannot say that he has seen electricity. He can only say that he has seen a pure expression of it. In the same way, man's behavior was intended by God to be a pure expression of His divine nature, though He remains unseen, and a man can no more produce this effect of *himself* than a bulb can produce light of *itself!* Try, and he will soon be exhausted, and at best he will only produce a shabby imitation of the real thing. It may impress him, but it certainly will not impress anyone else!

It is only the Spirit of God acting within a man who can ever enable him to behave as God intended a person to behave. "His divine power has granted to us all things that pertain to life and godliness, through the knowledge of him who called us to his own glory and excellence" (2 Pet. 1:3). His divine power is all that it takes for man to be godly—*but it takes nothing less!*

In other words, it takes God to be a *man!*

Man, that is, as God intended man to be. God created man to be inhabited *by* God *for* God! "In him was life, and the life was the light of men" (John 1:4). The light depended on the life.

Once the life was removed, the light went out, for the one was the consequence of the other, and man was plunged into the abysmal darkness of his own spiritual bankruptcy! What happened to the image of God in man? Without a *cause* there was no *effect*, and the attributes of godliness gave way to the anarchy of godlessness! "God looks down from heaven on the children of man to see if there are any who understand, who seek after God. They have all fallen away; together they have become corrupt; there is none who does good, not even one" (Ps. 53:2–3).

That is why a spiritual regeneration, or new birth— "renewal of the Holy Spirit" (Titus 3:5)—is absolutely imperative if man is to "put on the new nature (the regenerate self) created in God's image, [Godlike] in true righteousness and holiness" (Eph. 4:24, AMP).

Another Aspect of the Mystery: God Cannot Be Tempted

"Let no one say when he is tempted, 'I am being tempted by God,' for God cannot be tempted with evil, and he himself tempts no one" (James 1:13). If God cannot be tempted with evil, and Jesus Christ was God, how could He be tempted? "For we do not have a high priest who is unable to sympathize with our weaknesses, but one who in every respect has been tempted as we are, yet without sin" (Heb. 4:15).

It is no explanation to suggest that though *tempted* the Lord Jesus Christ was not tempted with *evil* but only tested—for the statement "yet without sin" clearly indicates that the nature of His temptation was such that it would have led to sin had it not been resisted. Indeed, we may safely assume that the temptations were as sinister and wicked and painful as anything that the devil could devise, and for this very reason "because he himself has suffered when tempted, he is able to help those who are being tempted" (2:18).

This then is also part of the mystery of godliness: that inherent in His willingness to be made man was the willingness of the Lord Jesus Christ to be made subject to temptation. For strange as it may seem, inherent in man's capacity to be godly is man's very capacity to sin! This may not at first be obvious, but we shall return to it at the appropriate time.

In the meantime, we are left with no alternative but to recognize the fact that it was not as *God* that Christ was tempted but as *man*—that the limitations inherent in His ability to be tempted were the same limitations He had so willingly accepted as being inherent in His ability, though Creator, to play the role of man as a creature and thereby become the visible representation of the Invisible.

It has been shown that the primary limitation imposed upon man, in order that he may be in the likeness of his Maker and bear the image of the Invisible, is that of total dependence upon God—that man's behavior, to be godly, must derive directly and exclusively from God's activity in him and through him. Any activity therefore in which a man may engage, no matter how nobly conceived, that does not stem from this humble attitude of dependence upon God violates the basic principles of man's true humanity and the role for which he was created. By independence (or the absence of faith) he eliminates *God* and substitutes *himself* to become both cause and effect—the source of his own "godliness." But only God has the right to be the source of His own godliness, so however unwittingly, such a man is acting as his own god!

This man will still believe or pretend that he is worshiping God, but as the object of his imitation, even Christ Himself may only be an excuse for man worshiping his own ability to imitate—an ability vested in himself. This is the basis of all self-righteousness!

It is startling to discover that even God may be used as an excuse for worshiping oneself, and this demonstrates again the satanic genius for distorting truth and deceiving man—for it was to this temptation that Adam and Eve fell in the garden!

Satan said, "God knows that when you eat of [the fruit] your eyes will be opened, and you will be like God, knowing good and evil" (Gen. 3:5). Satan succeeded in introducing into human experience an attitude toward God that he himself had already adopted, one of arrogant self-sufficiency, at once hostile to God, repudiating both the indispensability of the Creator to the creature and the moral responsibility of the creature to the Creator.   .

In so many words, Satan persuaded man that he could be Godlike without being God-conscious, that he had an adequate capacity in himself for being good without the necessity of having *God*, that he could be righteous in his own right and *morally adult* without the need of being *spiritually alive!* In short, he persuaded man that he could be independent—both cause and effect!

Revelation 4:11 declares, "Worthy are you, our Lord and God, to receive glory and honor and power, for you created all things, and by your will they existed and were created." If, then, man is to be true to the purpose of his creation, his primary responsibility will be to please God; but the Bible declares emphatically that "without faith it is impossible to please him" (Heb. 11:6). So the first requirement in man, if he is to please God, is *faith.*

Faith involves something more than an academic nod. It involves that total dependence upon God that produces divine action in man. Perhaps you may say, "Very well, I understand that faith is essential for those preoccupied with pleasing God, but I am *not* preoccupied with pleasing God! I do not wish to *displease* God, nor do I wish militantly to *oppose* Him. Frankly, I am disinterested! In my particular way of life, to me and to the circle in which I live and to the ambitions that I cherish, He is simply irrelevant. So far as God is concerned, I intend to maintain a passive neutrality!"

This, of course, is a sheer impossibility! Created for a specific purpose, you cannot adopt an attitude of neutrality toward the God who made you without being morally irre-responsible. God is not optional, God is an imperative! For this reason faith is not optional—faith is also an imperative! You either implement the purpose of your creation by dependence upon God, or you prostitute your humanity! "Whatever does not proceed from faith is sin" (14:23).

The facts of the case are transparently clear: you were created to please God! Without faith it is impossible for you to please Him, so without faith, whatever you do, no matter what it may be, is sin! The only alternative to faith is sin!

That is why Satan will always present you with a reason-able alternative to faith, for he knows that if only he can get you to act other than in dependence upon God, you will be defying your Creator, no matter how lofty your motives or otherwise commendable your actions.

Of the One who came to be perfect man, we read, "Christ did not please himself" (Rom. 15:3). As God, the Lord Jesus Christ had the right to please Himself, but as man He did not have that right. Whom then did He please? He pleased the Father! "I always do the things that are pleasing to him" (John 8:29).

So that at the end of thirty years, before Christ's baptism by John, and again during His public ministry, the Father could look down from heaven and say, "This is my beloved Son, with whom I am well pleased" (Matt. 3:17; 17:5). For Christ to have acted other than in dependence upon the Father would have vi-olated the perfection of His own humanity. That is why Satan's attacks upon the Son were designed to trick Him, somehow, into acting on His own initiative. But though tempted again and again, and in all points as we are, He was without sin. He never once acted other than in dependence on the Father.

One More Aspect of the Mystery: God Cannot Be Taught

God is answerable to no one but Himself, for He is the Omnipotent Creator. "Who are you, O man, to answer back to God? Will what is molded say to its molder, 'Why have you made me like this?'" (Rom. 9:20). God's authority is final, and He obeys no one, for to obey would be less than an act of God. "Before me no god was formed, nor shall there be any after me. I, I am the LORD, and besides me there is no Savior" (Isa. 43:10–11). Yet herein is the "foolishness" and the "weakness" of God (1 Cor. 1:25): that the Word, who was in the beginning with God and was God and by whom all things were made (see John 1:1–3) and "in whom are hidden all the treasures of wisdom and knowledge" and "who is the head of all rule and authority" (Col. 2:3, 10), should come into this world for your sake and mine and do what as God He had never done—He learned to obey! He entered the school of obedience, for "although he was a son, he learned obedience through what he suffered" (Heb. 5:8).

Was it possible for God to be in the school of obedience?

Only if as God He was prepared to behave as man! Had the Lord Jesus Christ on earth not only been God but also behaved as God, not only would no one have seen Him, and not only would it have been impossible for Him to be tempted, but it would have been impossible for Him to obey. But because He was willing to be God and behave as man at one and the same time, He was able to say, "I have not spoken on my own authority, but the Father who sent me has himself given me a commandment—what to say and what to speak" (John 12:49). As the sent One, the Son placed Himself at the disposal of, and submitted Himself in total obedience to, the

Sender, His Father, and "carried His obedience to the extreme of death, even the death of the cross!" (Phil. 2:8, AMP).

He was willing to "taste death for everyone" (Heb. 2:9) and suffer as man for men what would otherwise have been impossible for Him to suffer as God behaving as God, for God can never die.

God, "the King of the ages," is not only invisible, He is immortal (1 Tim. 1:17), "in the sense of exemption from every kind of death" (6:16, AMP). But of the Lord Jesus Christ, the Son, it is written,

> Both He Who sanctifies [making men holy] and those who are sanctified all have one [Father]. For this reason He is not ashamed to call them brethren. . . . Since, therefore, [these His] children share in flesh and blood [in the physical nature of human beings], He [Himself] in a similar manner partook of the same [nature], that by [going through] death He might bring to nought and make of no effect him who had the power of death—that is, the devil. (Heb. 2:11, 14, AMP)

In this amazing way our wonderful Redeemer, though never less than our Creator God, by His miraculous incarnation "emptied himself. . . . And being found in human form, he humbled himself by becoming obedient to the point of death" (Phil. 2:7–8). And He says to you and to me now, "As the Father has sent me, even so I am sending you" (John 20:21)—to learn to obey in the school of obedience and to enter into all the unspeakable privileges and blessings inherent in the *mystery of godliness.*

5

The Nature of a Man

May the God of peace himself sanctify you completely, and may your whole spirit and soul and body be kept blameless at the coming of our Lord Jesus Christ.
1 Thessalonians 5:23

It takes God to be a man, and godliness is the consequence of God's capacity to reproduce Himself in you!

In the light of these facts, it is necessary for us to examine the nature of man—to discover how he has been made and with what equipment he has been endowed that makes it *possible* for God to reproduce Himself in him. I am going to ask you to do a little "grunt work" with me in exposing some of the basic facts of man's humanity. If we are to place ourselves at God's disposal so that we may be used intelligently for the purpose for which we have been created, then we need to know something about ourselves.

"Sanctification" is not a tight-lipped expression of piety dressed in black lace and a bonnet, so heavenly that it is of no earthly use. To be sanctified means that God is able to put us completely to our correct use, and only when this is the case are we truly sanctified.

For the sake of simplicity, we are going to base our considerations upon the threefold description given to us by the Holy Spirit through the apostle Paul in First Thessalonians 5:23: "May the God of peace himself sanctify you completely, and may your whole spirit and soul and body be kept blameless at the coming of our Lord Jesus Christ."

Quite obviously this description presents man as a trinity—"spirit and soul and body"—and this is called a trichotomy. I am fully aware that there are many earnest folk who prefer to think of man as consisting only of two parts: a tangible part, the body, and an intangible part, the soul and the spirit lumped together as an indivisible entity. This is called a dichotomy.

It will not be my purpose to engage in any kind of theological controversy, for in this, as in so many other similar matters, there is truth in both suppositions, as there is truth to both sides of a coin. No matter how it falls, a nickel is worth a nickel, and you do not need to fight over which side is up—unless your game depends upon the toss!

To the fact that the body is tangible and that both soul and spirit are intangible I readily agree, and in this sense I am a dichotomist; but that the Bible deliberately discerns between soul and spirit is to me equally indisputable, and in this sense I am a trichotomist!

> The Word that God speaks is alive and full of power [making it active, operative, energizing and effective]; it is sharper than any two-edged sword, penetrating to the dividing line of the breath of life (soul) and [the immortal] spirit, and of joints and marrow [of the deepest parts of our nature], exposing and sifting and analyzing and judging the very thoughts and purposes of the heart. (Heb. 4:12, AMP)

But what gives life to this trichotomy that is man?

The Bible declares that "the life of the flesh is in the blood" (Lev. 17:11; see also Gen. 9:4; Deut. 12:23). It is a physiological fact that the blood is manufactured in the marrow; and the marrow, this source of life, being of such paramount importance to the body as a whole, is buried and protected deep within the joints and the bones. The joints provide a unique "behavior mechanism" that gives expression to the life flowing throughout the body. But it is ultimately from the marrow that flows the life that *motivates the mechanism*.

This is a beautiful illustration given to us by the Holy Spirit. The joints (our soul) and the marrow (our spirit) are interdependent if they are both to function properly; the one is buried deep within the other. Together they form one entity. Yet each remains distinct; they may not safely part company, but the one must not be mistaken for the other.

The final paradox, however, is that the marrow itself lives only as there flows *through* it the very life that stems from it: the blood! "For the blood"—not the marrow—"is the life" (Deut. 12:23). This is why the blood is sacred in the Bible. It represents *the very life of God Himself*—the Spirit of God within the human spirit, as the blood flowing through and from the marrow, imparting the very life of God to the human spirit, from whence this life must flow to activate the "joints" within the human soul and produce that pattern of behavior that enables man to bear the image of the Invisible and to give expression to the indwelling, quickening, motivating life of God.

It takes *God* to be a *man*! I believe that you will find it of immense value and a source of great enlightenment to consider man as Paul describes him, "spirit and soul and body"—a complete trinity. Much that is otherwise confusing will become refreshingly clear, and large tracts of the Bible will become infinitely more meaningful.

The most important part of man is his spirit; that is why it comes first in Paul's description. The next important part of man is his soul, and the least, though not an unimportant part of him, is his body.

Man's Body: An Earthly House

In that the body is the most tangible part of our being and that with which we are best acquainted (having spent many hours admiring it in the mirror), it will be simplest for us to begin with this, the least important part of our humanity. The body given by God to man is described in Second Corinthians 5:1: "We know that if the tent that is our earthly home is destroyed, we have a building from God, a house not made with hands, eternal in the heavens." Your body is your "earthly house," your temporary dwelling place, and you do not know how long you are going to be "at home." One atom bomb, and a whole lot of people are going to find themselves "homeless"—without a body—and you do not need to wait for a bomb if you would like to walk in front of a bus!

All forms of created life, however, have a "house" to live in, whether vegetable, animal or man. Look out the window, and you will see many forms of created life, all of which have bodies, and you recognize them individually and specifically by the particular shapes of their bodies.

In your mind you say to yourself, "That's a tree—it lives in a tree house. And there's a boy—he lives in a boy house. But that's a dog—it lives in a dog house!" You know that a cow is not a carrot, and I would know you from a cat! We recognize each other individually as men by our own peculiar shapes—some more peculiar than others!

In common with all other forms of living creatures, we also possess that *physical* quality of life that enables us to grow and to reproduce. The tree in the garden was not always the size it is—nor were you the size you are! Some of us feel that our capacity to grow in certain directions is a privilege that we might acceptably be spared!

Our bodies too present us with a convenient means of intercommunication. The flowers invite their insect guests with exotic colors, scent and form, and a little nectar puts the final touch to their seductive art! No one could say that a nightingale fails to communicate, nor, for that matter, a flea!

My busy fingers commit to paper what before too long your eyes will read. And should good fortune so dictate, maybe our paths one day will cross, and by the exercise of my thoracic and abdominal muscles, I will cause the thoracic cavity of my chest to operate like a bellows, causing a draught of air to pass swiftly through my larynx and cause my vocal cords, all suitably controlled, to produce a series of vibrations in a multiplicity of wavelengths to be conveyed in their own turn through the atmosphere. These will be caught by a cup-shaped appendage on the side of your head, called the ear, directed toward the outer eardrum and conveyed by an intricate mechanism to the inner ear, there to stimulate the waiting nerve ends, which will dutifully communicate an impulse to a certain section of your brain, and you will know that I have said "Good morning!"

I will have communicated!

Maybe we will shake hands on the strength of it, and add physical communication to verbal communication, but in any case our bodies will have come in quite handy as a means of expression. There is, however, a marked difference between the animal and the vegetable kingdoms.

Man's Soul: Where How We Will Behave Is Determined

A tree does not get aggravated by a lot of little weeds in the garden nor frightened by a bull. That is one of the advantages of being a vegetable! At the same time, a tree does not fall in love with the young bush over the wall nor laugh when a big man falls through his deck chair. That is one of the *disadvantages* of being a vegetable! In other words, a vegetable does not behave. It has a body but no behavior mechanism that enables it to calculate, react or decide. This ability is peculiar to the animal kingdom and constitutes essentially the difference between an animal and a vegetable. The seat of all animal behavior is in the soul, and it is with this part of our humanity that we must now concern ourselves.

That man is an animal goes without saying! We eat and drink the animal way; we breathe and breed and bleed—and die—the animal way!

That man is not only animal will, I trust, become equally clear, but animal he is! Furthermore, even as fallen man, he is perfectly capable of behaving though spiritually destitute and completely "alienated from the life of God" (Eph. 4:18). His spiritual condition determines not whether he can behave but only how he will behave.

Do animals, then, have souls? The answer to this question is found simply in the first chapters of Genesis.

"To every beast of the earth and to every bird of the heavens and to everything that creeps on the earth, everything that has the breath of life, I have given every green plant for food" (Gen. 1:30). "The LORD God formed man of the dust of the ground, and breathed into his nostrils the breath of life; and man became a living soul" (2:7, KJV).

The expression used in the first verse quoted above, "everything that has the breath of life," as relating to "every beast of the earth and to every bird of the heavens and to everything that creeps on the earth" (the animal kingdom) in contrast to "every green plant" (the vegetable kingdom) is an expression that corresponds precisely to that found in the second verse quoted from Genesis 2:7 and referring to man: "man became a living soul." Exactly the same Hebrew word is used in both cases, though it is translated differently in the King James Version ("life" in 1:30 and "soul" in 2:7) and translated differently again as "creature" in Genesis 1:20, 21 and 24; in 2:19; and in 9:10, 12, 15 and 16. In every case it is the same Hebrew word, and it means "soul" as applied to man or animal throughout the whole Bible.

The soul, broadly speaking, is also a trinity—mind, emotion and will—and enables all forms of animal life to react mentally, emotionally and volitionally within the capacity limits with which each has been endowed by the Creator. A worm, for instance, is rather less intelligent than the average schoolboy and certainly less affectionate, but it can still find its way around!

You behave by the exercise of your will under the influence of your mind and your emotions, and this process does not in itself require any visible activity on the part of the body. Your body is only required when you wish to give outward expression to your inward behavior—in other words, when you wish to communicate with your external circumstances.

And the way in which you ultimately communicate by physical activity may far from represent your true internal behavior! "His speech was smooth as butter [external behavior], yet war was in his heart [internal behavior]; his words were softer than oil, yet they were drawn swords" (Ps. 55:21).

Do you get the point? You said to him, "You're welcome"— but in your heart you could have strangled him!

When last did you sit in church with your body neatly propped against the back of the seat and your gaze politely set in the preacher's direction, while all the time you were visiting with someone fifty miles away? How many heated verbal exchanges have you had with some absent foe while standing at the kitchen sink—and you never uttered a word!

What exciting moments you have had and what frightening adventures—lying fast asleep upon your bed! Some of the best sermons I ever preached I preached in bed! A pity only that on these rare occasions of unusual eloquence, it was the preacher himself who slept—and not the congregation!

Psychiatrists declare that far more damage can be done and far deeper impressions made upon the character by this unseen behavior of the soul unmatched by physical action than by the actual outward deeds themselves. The fascination of the cinema, of watching television, of soaking in a novel or of scanning the many crime reports that fill the daily newspapers is that the unsuspecting victim of this process "lives" the part of the chosen character in the innermost recesses of the mind and emotions, thereby satisfying some inward urge to be a hero, attracting attention to himself, wreaking some awful vengeance upon unkind society, indulging some illicit lust or fulfilling such ignoble ambitions in the secret of the soul as might otherwise be incompatible, if performed, with the impression he would like to give to others of himself!

> The thoughts of the wicked are an abomination to the LORD. (Prov. 15:26)

> As he thinketh in his heart, so is he. (23:7, KJV)

> Everyone who hates his brother is a murderer. (1 John 3:15)

> Everyone who looks at a woman with lustful intent has already committed adultery with her in his heart. (Matt. 5:28)

Fortunately, this activity within the soul can be as beneficial as it can be damaging, nourishing nobility of character and making such indelible impressions as may shape our future ends. These lofty deeds are first cradled in the soul and later clothed with action in the light of day! It was with this in mind that Paul wrote to the Philippian church,

> Whatever is true, whatever is honorable, whatever is just, whatever is pure, whatever is lovely, whatever is commendable, if there is any excellence, if there is anything worthy of praise, think about these things. (4:8)

Paul knew that to "*think about these things*" would inevitably provide the "dress rehearsal" for the believers' ultimate performance, profoundly affecting their behavior from within and from without.

The behavior process of the soul may be protracted and leisurely. On the other hand, it can take place with amazing rapidity and be matched almost instantly with the appropriate physical action, as when a driver in an emergency applies his brakes and swerves to a grinding halt, a fielder leaps to catch a ball and win a game, or some bodyguard throws himself in a split second between his master and the deadly missile of his murderous assassin. Supposing you became very angry with me and highly excited—your emotions thus disturbed might well say to your will, "Hit him!" And if your emotions dominated your will, what would you do? You would hit me! Probably, however, in the meantime, your mind—acting on information received through your eyes—would say to your will, "Don't do that! He's bigger than you are—and he will hit you back!" This is how you function thousands of times a day. You look at your watch, and the mind says to the will, "It's time to go!" and the will says to the legs, "Quick march!" and off you go!

Perhaps, however, your watch is slow. No matter, then, how sincere your mind may be in the conclusions drawn from the false information provided by the watch—you will be sincerely wrong! The train will have gone!

Having believed what you heard about a certain person, your emotional reactions toward that individual may be adversely affected—and what you heard may well have been a wicked lie!

Quite obviously, if your mental conclusions and your emotional attitudes are to be not only quite sincere but right, they must derive from truth! Your morality may be determined by the degree to which your will responds to right mental conclusions and to right emotional reactions and translates these influences into positive action.

The basis, therefore, of all true morality is truth! The Bible makes it abundantly clear that truth is expressed through the Word:

In many separate revelations [each of which set forth a portion of the Truth] and in different ways God spoke of old to [our] forefathers in and by the prophets, [but] in the last of these days He has spoken to us in [the person of a] Son. (Heb. 1:1–2, AMP)

Words are essentially a means of communicating information, and the information conveyed will affect the behavior of the recipient to the degree in which he acts upon it. When you act in strict obedience to the truth revealed through the Word, the truth behaves, and the end effect is righteousness!

As the absolute Source of truth revealed through the Word, God is the absolute Source of righteousness. Satan, on the other hand, as the absolute source of all that is false, is the absolute source of all unrighteousness. The first word he ever spoke to man was a lie, and he has been deceiving him ever since. He "masquerades as an angel of light" (2 Cor. 11:14, AMP) and propagates his malicious lies through those of his dupes who "by smooth talk and flattery . . . deceive the hearts of the naive" (Rom. 16:18).

It is interesting to note that only man within the animal kingdom is capable of producing words and of recognizing them to any great extent in order to convey and receive exact items of information. In other words, only man can hear and utter—or distort—the truth! Maybe his capacity for speech plays a far bigger part than we had thought in man's capacity to behave as a moral being. It lays him open to the Word!

Monkeys chatter in the trees and dogs may bark at cats, but though it may be very meaningful to them, what they have to say is somewhat ungrammatical! Even if the parrot can say "Pretty Polly" or "Kiss me, darling," it has only learned to copy certain sounds—no message is conveyed. What added complications would result for all mankind if once our poor dumb friends could get together and discuss the stupidity and wickedness of men! What lies our tabby cat might tell the cat next door about the way we live at home! Let this then be our consolation—if these lesser creatures cannot know the truth, neither can they very well distort it!

Notwithstanding this, neither animal nor man needs any particular relationship to God just simply to behave. If you own a dog, when you get home, does he not recognize you as his master, wag his tail and run to meet you, indicating with his muddy paws all down your front how pleased he is to see you? The dog does not object when you enter the house through the front door; he knows that you have the right, because you live there. But what if someone climbs through the bathroom window at three o'clock in the morning? The dog would think to himself, *My master doesn't usually come through the bathroom window at three in the morning—not often!* Then, after suitable investigation, sufficient to satisfy himself that the shape of the body does not correspond with that of any friend of the family as previously recorded in his memory, the faithful dog would discharge his responsibilities by indicating his distinct displeasure through the use of the sharper end of his anatomy, probably to the detriment of the intruder's pants!

Take the dog for a walk, and when he strays too far, you call him; then, standing in the distance, head on one side with one ear up and the other ear down and with a mischievous grin on his face, the dog will hesitate. *What shall I do? Shall I obey? Or chase the cat? The latter would be far more interesting!* Then you shout a little louder and with some impatience in your voice, and the dog remembers what happened last time he disobeyed you—and it hurt! So he comes to heel, tail half between his legs, and just far enough away from you to be safe!

All this behavior has in the first instance taken place within the soul of the dog, and the muddy paw marks on your trousers indicate that on your arrival home the dog "functioned"—communicating to you his mental recognition and his emotional delight by translating them into volitional action, having used his body to run through the dirtiest puddle he can find and then jumping up to greet you!

I was staying on the east coast of New England some years ago, and my hostess explained the great dilemma in which she had found herself in her desire to feed both birds and squirrels at one and the same time. She had discovered that the squirrels had the unhappy knack of getting all that she provided for the birds, and she had used all her ingenuity to discover a means whereby she could segregate their appetites.

Then she hit on the master plan! From the second story of her home, there was a laundry line that ran out over a pulley to a distant tree over a lawn, and so, taking about two yards of fine thread and the lid of a tin to act as a small tray, she placed the peanut butter on the lid and suspended it from the clothesline with the thread and pulled it out halfway between the house and the tree. That was for the birds, and no squirrel could get at it!

My hostess went on to explain that only a matter of minutes later, as she looked out the window, she saw a squirrel run up the trunk of the tree, climb upside down along the laundry line, hang by its hind legs over the tray, pull the tray up by the thread with its front paws and eat the peanut butter! Then, dropping the tin lid, the squirrel returned by the same route to the tree with a big, satisfied grin on its face. That was not just instinct—as far as my hostess was concerned, it was not even funny! It was cold calculation, brilliantly executed—and still outwitted by the squirrels, this good lady has given up trying to feed the birds.

We may understand, therefore, that if all that we consist of is body and soul, then man is nothing more than a clever animal. And the natural man, in his unregenerate condition, behaves as if this were so. He busies himself primarily with "servicing" the body and to this end goes out to work to earn his daily bread and such other luxuries as will add to the comfort or pleasurable use of his body. He is only vaguely aware that he has a soul but somehow recognizes that he must "keep body and soul together," otherwise his kindly relatives will come and bury the body!

This is not irrelevant to the times in which we live, for although we may not discuss the matter within the compass of this book, the hypothesis that man is nothing more than the highest form of animal life as yet developed on this particular planet lies at the very heart of Christless, godless and God-hating communism. This is the very basis upon which the theory of atheistic dialectic materialism is founded—a philosophy admirably suited to clothe that satanic attitude of arrogant self-sufficiency, which we saw in chapter 4 to be the very essence of the attitude introduced by the devil into human experience at the Fall, repudiating both the indispensability of the Creator to the creature and the moral responsibility of the creature to the Creator.

According to this supposition, not only does man cease to be morally responsible, but he has no eternal destiny; when he dies, he dies like a dog, forfeiting thereby only animal existence. Little wonder, therefore, that life on the other side of the Iron Curtain is held to be so cheap! We are threatened today on every side, from within and from without, by this wicked philosophy of human existence, and we need to know why it is that we consider ourselves to be men as distinct from mere animals and not just animals that happen to be called men.

Man's Spirit: The Place in Which God Can Dwell

What is the essential difference between man as man and the rest of the animal kingdom? God has given to man what He has not given to any other form of created life: the human spirit. This, though intrinsically indivisible from the human soul, must not be mistaken for the human soul. As the marrow within the joints, so is the human spirit buried deep within the human soul, remaining essentially distinct yet together with the soul forming that complete immaterial entity capable of endless survival after physical death. This is opposed to the purely animal soul common to the rest of the animal kingdom, which possesses no such capacity either to survive or to be held morally responsible beyond the grave.

This capacity for endless survival beyond physical death must not be confused with immortality, which is a characteristic, strictly speaking, of God alone:

> I charge you in the presence of God, who gives life to all things ["preserves alive all living things," AMP], and of Christ Jesus, who in his testimony before Pontius Pilate made the good confession, . . . he who is the blessed and only Sovereign, the King of kings and Lord of lords, who alone has immortality ["in the sense of exemption from every kind of death," AMP]. (1 Tim. 6:13–16)

In God and God alone is life eternally inherent—eternally *pre*-existent, *self*-existent and self-*perpetuating*—and this characteristic of deity is shared equally by the Son, the Lord Jesus Christ, with the Father and with the "eternal Spirit" (Heb. 9:14). "For even as the Father has life in Himself and is self-existent, so He has given to the Son to have life in Himself and be self-existent" (John 5:26, AMP).

It is for this reason that God is absolute, self-sufficient and completely independent. All other forms of life, vegetable, animal, spiritual or angelic, are essentially derived and not self-existent, and they remain dependent upon the Creator as the One who is the only Source and the only Sustainer of all life:

> The God who made the world and everything in it, being Lord of heaven and earth, does not live in temples made by man; nor is he served by human hands, as though he needed anything, since he himself gives to all mankind life and breath and everything. . . . "In him we live and move and have our being." (Acts 17:24–25, 28)

> In his hand is the life of every living thing and the breath of all mankind. (Job 12:10)

> The God in whose hand is your breath, and whose are all your ways, you have not honored. (Dan. 5:23)

To quote the late Archdeacon T.C. Hammond, M.A., one-time principal of Moore Theological College, Sydney, Australia, "Immortality does not merely mean endless 'survival,' but 'eternal life.' It is its quality which is important. Whilst the souls of the unregenerate will survive the disintegration of the body, only the regenerate can experience the life—which is of the same quality as the Divine Life—which has been 'brought to light' through the Gospel"[1] (see 2 Tim. 1:10).

The human spirit is this unique capacity that God has given to man that enables him both to receive and to be motivated by the very life of God Himself. To return to my illustration of chapter 4, the human spirit is the lamp, incapable itself of producing light but capable of receiving that which working in and through it produces light and upon which it must be constantly dependent if it is to fulfill the purpose for which, as a lamp, it was created. "The spirit of man is the lamp of the LORD" (Prov. 20:27).

As translated in the King James Version of Proverbs 20:20, the word "candle" means "lamp," and what the electricity is to an electric lamp and oil is to an oil lamp the Holy Spirit is to the human spirit. With relentless consistency throughout the Scriptures, oil represents the person and office of the Holy Spirit, in whose person God is able to inhabit man's humanity and make him a partaker of His own divine nature. By this indwelling man may be not only physically alive, as an animal, but spiritually alive, like God:

> Thus says the One who is high and lifted up, who inhabits eternity, whose name is Holy: "I dwell in the high and holy place, and also with him who is of a contrite and lowly spirit, to revive the spirit of the lowly, and to revive the heart of the contrite. (Isa. 57:15)

> He has granted to us his precious and very great promises, so that through them you may become partakers of the divine nature. (2 Pet. 1:4)

It is man's capacity to receive God and to enjoy God and to be enjoyed by God that makes him man as opposed to mere animal, and it is only God in man that enables him to function as God intended man to function.

Lose God, and man loses everything that truly makes him man and enables him to behave as God intended man to behave. The anarchy of godlessness begins! The human spirit destitute of the Holy Spirit leaves the soul abandoned as a ship without a rudder on a storm-tossed sea, spiritually bankrupt, dead, "alienated from the life of God" (Eph. 4:18)—an easy prey to every evil, malicious and malevolent influence of which it may fall foul!

This has been the unhappy lot of man since Adam made his fateful choice. To rescue him God sent His Son—to make man man again. Man as God intended man to be!

"I will not contend forever, neither will I be angry always, for [if I did stay angry] the spirit [of man] would faint and be consumed before Me, and [My purpose in] creating the souls of men would be frustrated" (Isa. 57:16, AMP).

6

The First Man Adam

Thus it is written, "The first man Adam became a living being."
1 Corinthians 15:45

Thank you for the "grunt work" of the preceding chapter. I trust that you are still with me! We saw that when man acts in strict obedience to the truth, the truth behaves, and the result is righteousness: "conformity to the divine will in thought, purpose, and action" (Rom. 6:18, AMP). We saw as well that the truth is communicated through the Word, having its absolute source in God: "Every gift which is good, and every perfect boon, is from above, and comes down from the Father, who is the source of all Light. In Him there is no variation nor the slightest suggestion of change" (James 1:17, WEY).

We also saw, as we considered the nature of man, that the human spirit is that part of man created to be inhabited by the Holy Spirit. The purpose of this indwelling is that man might exercise his will under the influence of a God-taught mind and God-controlled emotions to the exclusion of all other alien influences that would deflect him from conformity to the divine will in thought, purpose or action.

Adam in His Innocency

In his innocency and before the Fall, the first man Adam acted consistently under the gracious and exclusive influence of the truth from within him, being inhabited by God Himself. By partaking of and being motivated by the divine nature, he was lifted beyond mere animal status and behavior into the noble vocation of manhood and human behavior. He was altogether Godlike because all his faculties were placed unreservedly at God's disposal.

To clarify this further, allow me to take a few moments to explain the chart on the next page.

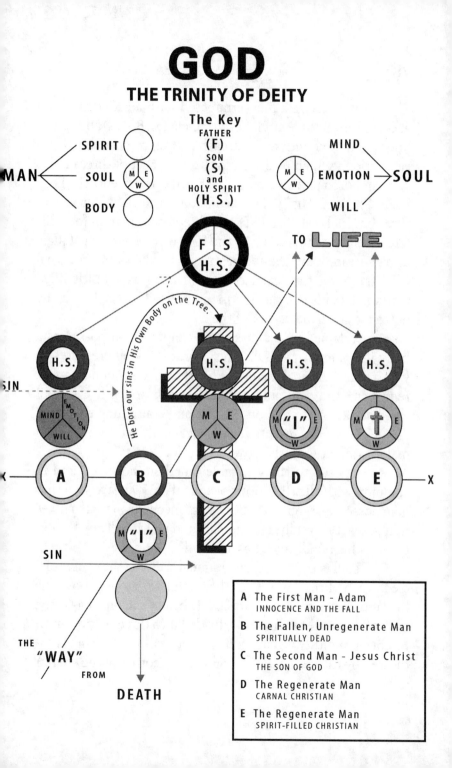

GOD
THE TRINITY OF DEITY

The Key
FATHER
(F)
SON
(S)
and
HOLY SPIRIT
(H.S.)

MAN — SPIRIT / SOUL / BODY

MIND / EMOTION / WILL → SOUL

TO LIFE

He bore our sins in His Own Body on the Tree.

SIN

A — B — C — D — E — X

SIN

THE "WAY" FROM

DEATH

A The First Man - Adam
INNOCENCE AND THE FALL

B The Fallen, Unregenerate Man
SPIRITUALLY DEAD

C The Second Man - Jesus Christ
THE SON OF GOD

D The Regenerate Man
CARNAL CHRISTIAN

E The Regenerate Man
SPIRIT-FILLED CHRISTIAN

You will notice a line terminated with an X at each end and five sets of three circles each, labeled A, B, C, D and E. The line terminated with an X at each end represents the physical world in which we live, and the center set of three circles superimposed upon a cross and labeled C represents the Lord Jesus Christ in His perfect manhood. The other four sets of three circles labeled A, B, D and E represent man in four different relationships to God: the first man, Adam; the fallen, unregenerate man; the regenerate man who is but a carnal Christian; and the regenerate man living as a Spirit-filled Christian. (This is indicated in more detail by the key at the bottom right-hand corner of the chart.)

As explained in the preceding chapter, man possesses a body in common with all other forms of living creatures as well as that physical quality of life that enables him to grow, reproduce and communicate. So in each of the five sets of three circles, the circle on the line and containing the letter A, B, C, D or E represents the physical body with which man makes contact with the physical world.

As opposed to the vegetable kingdom, however, and in common with all other forms of animal life, we have seen that man possesses a soul—that behavior mechanism that enables him to react mentally, emotionally and volitionally by the exercise of his mind, emotions and will.

The soul is portrayed diagrammatically by the center circle in each of the five sets of three circles; four are above the line and, in the case of figure B, one below the line. Basically, each of these center circles is divided into three sections representing mind (M), emotion (E) and will (W). (This is indicated by the key at the top right-hand corner of the chart.)

The presence of the capital I in the circles representing the soul in figures B and D and of the cross in the circle representing the soul in figure E will be explained more fully later in this and in succeeding chapters of the book.

In chapter 5 it was clearly demonstrated that what distinguishes man from the animal kingdom is that he possesses a human spirit—the "lamp of the LORD" (Prov. 20:27)—this unique capacity that enables him both to receive and to be motivated by the very life of God Himself. In the chart, the third circle in each of the five sets of three represents the human spirit—the highest of the three circles in each case except in that of figure B, where it is the lowest.

Thus by each set of three circles, extending either above the line as in figures A, C, D and E or below the line as in figure B, the whole man is represented—spirit, soul and body. (This is indicated by the key at the top left-hand corner of the chart.)

Furthermore, above the figures A, B, C, D and E, God is represented in the Trinity of Deity by the larger circle subdivided into three sections representing the Father (F), the Son (S) and the Holy Spirit (H.S.). The Holy Spirit's presence is also indicated in the top circles of figures A, C, D and E.

Having become familiar with the illustration, let us now consider Adam in his innocency. Figure A represents the first man, Adam, before the Fall. I would like you to consider this matter with me for several moments, bearing in mind that to commit spiritual issues to paper in diagrammatic form must inevitably involve a certain amount of over-simplification.

You will notice in figure A that the human spirit of the first man Adam is shown with a smaller circle within it, marked H.S. and representing the Holy Spirit. Though this in itself may be the first over-simplification, I believe this description to be legitimate, and I know of no better way of indicating the indisputable fact that God created man to be not only physically but also spiritually alive.

When God gave to Adam the solemn warning "In the day that you eat of it you shall surely die" (Gen. 2:17), it is quite obvious that He was not referring to physical death as the first consequence of sin, though this did become a secondary consequence. God was referring to spiritual death, and it is equally obvious that Adam was capable of spiritual death while remaining physically alive, a fact constantly asserted in the New Testament. To the redeemed, Paul writes, "Present yourselves to God as those who have been brought from death to life" (Rom. 6:13), and "You He made alive, who were dead in trespasses and sins" (Eph. 2:1, NKJV), for a Christian is literally a person who has been raised spiritually from the dead.

Apart from life, however, death is meaningless! You can say of a piece of wood, "It's dead!" but not of a lump of clay. Clay has no capacity for life, and therefore cannot die—it cannot forfeit what it does not have. Death is what is left when the life that should be there is absent! If Adam was capable of death while remaining physically alive, it can only mean that he possessed originally, in his innocency, a quality of life other than physical, which under certain circumstances he could forfeit without forfeiting physical life.

What was the life that Adam forfeited? It was spiritual life—the very life of God Himself:

> In the beginning was the Word, and the Word was with God, and the Word was God. He was in the beginning with God. All things were made through him. . . . In him was life, and the life was the light of men. (John 1:1-4)

When the life went out, the light went out!

When the Lord Jesus Christ raised Lazarus from the dead, how did He do it? He simply restored to his body the physical life that his body had forfeited and without which his body could only rot. What happens spiritually when a sinner turns to Christ and his sins are forgiven? Paul says, "As in Adam all die, so also in Christ shall all be made alive" (1 Cor. 15:22). Raised from the dead! "He made us alive together in fellowship and in union with Christ; [He gave us the very life of Christ Himself, the same new life with which He quickened Him]" (Eph. 2:5, AMP). Raised from the dead!

As the raising of Lazarus from the dead involved the restoration to him of the quality of life that he had forfeited—physical life—so it is reasonable to suppose that being spiritually raised from the dead involves the restoration to man of that quality of life that he forfeited by the Fall—spiritual life. The life restored in resurrection must be the same kind of life that was forfeited in death!

How then is spiritual life restored to those who are redeemed? We know that it is by the presence of the Holy Spirit:

> When the goodness of God our Saviour, and His love to man, dawned upon us, not in consequence of things which we, as righteous men, had done, but as a result of His own mercy He saved us by means of the bath of regeneration and renewal of our natures by the Holy Spirit, which He poured out on us richly through Jesus Christ our Saviour. (Titus 3:4–6, WEY)

> May [he] grant you to be strengthened with power through his Spirit in your inner being. (Eph. 3:16)

> Do you not know that you are God's temple and that God's Spirit dwells in you? (1 Cor. 3:16)

If, therefore, spiritual life is restored by the presence of the Holy Spirit, it is a reasonable supposition that spiritual death took place by the forfeiture of the presence of the Holy Spirit. Furthermore, as already discussed in the first chapter, when here on earth, the Lord Jesus Christ did not play the part of fallen man, nor did He demonstrate only the role of regenerate man—He came simply to be man as He as Creator had created him, with all the privileges and all the limitations involved—and as man He lived constantly by the Father through the Holy Spirit. Is it not safe to assume, therefore, that the first man Adam in his innocency enjoyed the life of God through the Holy Spirit even as the Lord Jesus as man enjoyed the life of the Father through the Holy Spirit—and as every redeemed sinner is renewed with the life of God through the Holy Spirit?

I have taken time to consider this matter with you at some length, because in the absence of chapter and verse, you have the right to know by what process of reasoning the first man Adam, as represented in my figure A, is shown as possessing the Holy Spirit within his human spirit.

There may be others who would wish to explain the matter differently, and I will not quarrel with them so long as it is clearly recognized that Adam in his innocency was not only physically but spiritually alive; that the spiritual life he possessed was the very life of God Himself, not inherent in Adam but derived from God and God-imparted; and that by the forfeiture of this life, Adam was capable of suffering a spiritual death that physically, both in the area of his soul and of his body, he could survive. This will be the sense in which I speak of Adam being indwelt by the Holy Spirit before he sinned.

Referring again to figure A, we see the human spirit of the first man Adam filled with the life of God through the presence of the Holy Spirit. Imagine now that this life floods his soul—his behavior mechanism—so that his mind is totally, unreservedly placed at the disposal of the Holy Spirit and his emotions are placed totally, unreservedly at the disposal of the Holy Spirit. Who now controls his will? The Holy Spirit—the Spirit of truth! Everything Adam does and every attitude he adopts will be an expression of the God who made him, who lives within him and expresses Himself through him. He becomes the "brightness of His glory" and the "express image of his person"—Godlike not by imitation but by allowing God to behave through him.

Had we been given the opportunity at that time of watching Adam in action, we would have seen a perfect image of God expressing His nature and His character, but God Himself would still have remained invisible. This image of God is represented in the diagram by the gray margin at the circumference of the circle representing the body, for as we have already seen, it is by physical activity that expression is given to the behavior processes of the soul, making visible to the world without what is invisible within.

As God made him in his innocency, Adam's external behavior in the body corresponded completely to his internal behavior in the soul, which in turn reflected exactly the gracious activity of the Holy Spirit. He was a lamp that was lit, fulfilling the purpose for which God had made him. It is quite obvious that if this process had been purely mechanical and Adam had possessed no capacity to exercise his own choice, he would have been no more than a robot—an impersonal "device" completely incapable of responding to or of satisfying the love of God. For only love can satisfy love, and love cannot be compelled! To win a person's friendship, you clasp his hand—you do not clench your fist. All genuine affection springs from free volition, and you cannot truly love without the power to choose.

A little girl will love her china doll because her imagination is vivid enough to imagine every kind of response: it answers back, it laughs and cries. It can be spanked when it is naughty, and it can be kissed when it is good! But there comes a day when the old china doll lies neglected, staring glassy-eyed in the corner of the cupboard—jettisoned for the lifeless thing it is. Nothing now but the real thing—for all the calls a child may make upon her time and patience—can ever satisfy a mother's love. And the supreme prize? To be loved back! And God is love!

Man was made to love God back—to reciprocate God's love to man. And Adam in his innocency, knowing that he had been created to please God and to bear His image, and knowing that he could only do so by maintaining an attitude of total dependence upon Him, expressed his love to God by total dependence on God! This was a faith-love relationship that could not help but express itself in total obedience, for obedience is the only logical consequence of faith.

If you give me your advice and I depend on it, then I will do as you say! This is the characteristic of faith as it is portrayed in the Bible. It involves an attitude toward God that always does what He says. And if you always do what He says, the world will see Him behaving through you—and that is godliness!

The picture then that we have of the first man Adam, before the image was marred, is of one whose love for God was demonstrated by his dependence on God, resulting in obedience to God. Indwelt by the life of God, controlled by the life of God and expressing the life of God! Spirit, soul and body wholly filled and flooded by God Himself.

> When I view and consider Your heavens, the work of Your fingers, the moon and the stars, which You have ordained and established, What is man that You are mindful of him, and the son of [earthborn] man that You care for him? Yet you have made him but little lower than God [or heavenly beings], and You have crowned him with glory and honor. You made him to have dominion over the works of Your hands; You have put all things under his feet. (Ps. 8:3–6, AMP)

Made by God to have dominion over all the works of His hands, man's authority was vested in him only by virtue of this faith-love relationship to God, which would keep him always conformed to the divine will in "purpose, thought, and action." He was to be the visible means of communication between an invisible God and His visible creation, whose sovereignty "over the works of [God's] hands" would be subject only to the sovereignty of God Himself.

This was the significance of the forbidden fruit! It was in this matter that Adam was to recognize the limits of his own authority and maintain his attitude of humble dependence upon his Maker, knowing that his own "dominion" derived from God alone. Given the moral capacity to choose, it was necessary for man to have a point at which choice could be exercised, and by humbly submitting to this divine prohibition at the tree in the garden, Adam was able both to affirm his desire to please God and at the same time acknowledge that his very life depended on Him. In this way his love toward God found tangible expression in the obedience of faith and qualified him to be the recipient of the divine life as the agent of the divine will. Adam had nothing to do with being alive spiritually—he was alive! God had made him that way.

The Conversion of Adam

Perhaps you did not know that Adam was converted. But he was, for conversion begins with a change of mind, and Adam changed his mind about God! He allowed the devil to poison his understanding, and believing a lie, *he died by faith!*

God had made it abundantly clear that the moment Adam repudiated his faith-love relationship toward Him, he would surely die, forfeiting the life of God that makes man man—for it takes God to be a man! Satan, as we saw in chapter 4, succeeded in persuading Adam that he could lose God and lose nothing—that he could exercise dominion over all the works of God's hands without subjecting himself to the demands of God's will. He would now be his own free agent, enjoying liberty of action in the area of his mind, his emotion and his will without the restrictive influence of the Spirit of God.

He was to trade dependence for independence! He was to throw out his own big chest, stick out his own big chin, stand on his own big feet and demonstrate the adequacy of a man without God! He acted on what he believed from the lips of a liar—and he died!

In figure A you will notice the introduction of the sin principle into human experience (the dotted arrow): "Sin came into the world through one man, and death through sin, and so death spread to all men because all sinned" (Rom. 5:12).

What happened? God had said, "In the day that you eat of [the forbidden fruit] you shall surely die" (Gen. 2:17). Did

Adam die in the day that he ate of the fruit? Not physically. The next morning when he awoke, the sky was still blue, the sun was still shining, and the birds were still singing in the trees! He could think with his mind, react with his emotions, and decide with his will. Body and soul, he still functioned! Physically alive and soulishly active, the animal part of him survived, but the very day that he repudiated his dependence on God, Adam forfeited the presence of God! He was dead! Only the shell remained, henceforth to be a monstrous parody of the real thing (figure B).

God had thrown the master switch, and the Holy Spirit had withdrawn from the human spirit. When the life went out, the light went out, and the soul of man was plunged into the abysmal darkness of a fallen humanity, uninhabited by God. Ever since Adam fell into sin, every child born into this world has been born in the pattern of fallen man: "by nature children of wrath, like the rest of mankind . . . darkened in their understanding, alienated from the life of God because of the ignorance that is in them, due to their hardness of heart" (Eph. 2:3; 4:18). Godlessness, lifelessness and lightlessness were the inevitable consequences of Adam's conversion. Of his own free volition he stepped out of dependence into independence, out of life into death, and out of light into darkness! He was on his own! At least he thought he was!

Figure B in the diagram shows the human spirit of fallen man (the lowest circle) now destitute of the Holy Spirit—sin has come between him and God. This in itself would have been bad enough, for in the absence of the motivating life of God, in terms of his behavior, man would simply have been reduced to the status of a very clever animal. For remember, being spiritually alive does not determine whether a man can behave but simply how he will behave. Even so, he might have been as harmless and as pleasant as a flock of sheep!

Something happened, however, even worse than the for-feiture of the presence of God. You will notice in figure B that a small circle has been introduced into the center circle representing the soul, and in the center of the smaller circle a capital I! From now on man is to be egocentric instead of Deo-centric—he has become an I specialist! This principle of egocentricity is called in the Bible "the flesh" (not to be con-fused with the human body; see Rom. 7:18; 8:3) and has its origin and roots in the devil himself. Another word used for this evil principle in the Bible is "sin," as opposed to "sins" (Rom. 7:14, 20; John 16:9), and yet again "the old self" (Rom. 6:6; Eph. 4:22; Col. 3:9) or "self" (see 2 Cor. 5:15).

In the absence of the Holy Spirit instructing and control-ling man's mind and emotions and will with truth, Satan, who is the father of lies (see John 8:44), invaded the soul of man, usurped the sovereignty of God, and introduced this evil agency to pollute, corrupt, abuse and misuse his soul. He so twisted and bent his will that the behavior mechanism in man, designed by God to be the means whereby he should bear the divine image, was prostituted by the devil to become the means whereby man would bear the satanic image, for "whoever makes a practice of sinning is of the devil" (1 John 3:8), or "takes his character from the evil one" (AMP). His body became an instrument of unrighteousness instead of being an instrument of righteousness. Thus man became infinitely worse than an animal, for emptied of his divine content, and his soul invaded by the flesh, the animal part of him became the plaything and the workshop of the devil himself.

Yet in spite of this unpleasant fact, to which human be-havior has given ample testimony all down the centuries, it is important to point out at this stage that even in his un-regenerate, fallen condition, man is still not just mere ani-mal, for there is still within him—though empty of God and spiritually dead—his human spirit. This, added to his soul (as the marrow to the joints), not only enables man, though unredeemed, to survive physical death and remain morally responsible to God but, before physical death, makes it pos-sible for a man to be spiritually regenerate by faith in Christ, no matter how degenerate he may have become.

To illustrate what I mean, supposing you were to hang potatoes from the ceiling of your sitting room in addition to the lamps already there. How much less light would you get from the potatoes than from your lamps, if you did not switch on the lamps? You would say, "No less light from the potatoes, for I would get no light from any of them, lamps or potatoes!" Exactly! Then why do you not use potatoes, if you get no less light from them—are they not cheaper than lamps? "Don't be so stupid!" you would say. "You can switch on a lamp, but you cannot switch on a potato!" Right again! A potato cannot receive what it takes to produce a light!

That is the essential difference between "the animal man" ("L'homme animal," 1 Cor. 2:14, Louis Segond French translation) and mere animal. The unregenerate man be-haves on the same principle that an animal behaves, and as we have seen, because of the flesh, far worse than an ani-mal, for he produces "the works of the flesh" (Gal. 5:19–21; see also Mark 7:20–23). But there remains within him the capacity to be "switched on again" by the "washing of re-generation and renewal of the Holy Spirit" (Titus 3:5) and so to be restored to his true humanity, if he will repent and receive Christ as his Savior. And "if anyone is in Christ, he is a new creation. The old has passed away; behold, the new has come" (2 Cor. 5:17).

By his conversion, therefore, the first man Adam not only lost the life of God and ceased to be in the image of God, but his whole personality became available to the devil to be exploited by him. This produced a race of men whose ungodly behavior, represented by the black margin at the circumference of circle B, is a demonstration of "the mystery of iniquity" (2 Thess. 2:7, KJV), or "that hidden principle of rebellion against constituted authority" (AMP).

> God's [holy] wrath and indignation are revealed from heaven against all ungodliness and unrighteousness of men, who in their wickedness repress and hinder the truth and make it inoperative. For that which is known about God is evident to them and made plain in their inner consciousness, because God [Himself] has shown it to them. For ever since the creation of the world His invisible nature and attributes, that is, His eternal power and divinity, have been made intelligible and clearly discernible in and through the things that have been made (His handiworks). So [men] are without excuse [altogether without any defense or justification]. Because when they knew and recognized Him as God, they did not honor and glorify Him as God or give Him thanks. But instead they became futile and godless in their thinking [with vain imaginings, foolish reasoning, and stupid speculations] and their senseless minds were darkened. Claiming to be wise, they became fools [professing to be smart, they made simpletons of themselves]. And by them the glory and majesty and

excellence of the immortal God were exchanged for and represented by images, resembling mortal man and birds and beasts and reptiles. (Rom. 1:18–23, AMP)

In other words, man was no longer anchored to anything absolute and so was at liberty to choose his own gods as the objects of his own imitation to suit his own convenience, satisfy his own unholy lusts, and feed his own incorrigible pride! "They exchanged the truth of God for a lie and worshiped and served the creature rather than the Creator, Who is blessed forever!" (1:25, AMP).

7

The Mystery of Iniquity

For the mystery of iniquity doth already work.
2 Thessalonians 2:7, KJV

When the Lord Jesus Christ turned to Peter and said, "Get behind me, Satan! You are a hindrance to me" (Matt. 16:23), He meant exactly what He said. He was talking to the devil! It was Peter who had spoken, but the Lord Jesus Christ knew perfectly well that it was Satan who was behaving, borrowing Peter's humanity as a means of expressing his malicious and subtle attempt to dissuade Christ from going to the cross. Peter's reasoning was sincere, and his emotional concern for his Master genuine, but the conclusions that he drew and the attitude that he adopted were false, for neither stemmed from truth!

The Lord Jesus Christ had already begun to show His disciples the truth about His messianic mission, "that he must go to Jerusalem and suffer many things from the elders and chief priests and scribes, and be killed, and on the third day be raised" (16:21). But Peter resisted the truth unwittingly under the evil influence of the flesh (that sin principle of satanic origin, always hostile to God and always opposed to truth), and what to Peter was a noble sentiment, "God forbid, Lord! This must never happen to You!" (Matt. 16:22, AMP), was recognized by Christ to be a wicked thrust from the devil himself as he sought to thwart the redemptive purpose of God. The devil knew that Calvary would be not only the place of his own defeat but the place where man would be rescued from his clutches and restored to his true humanity!

Little wonder, then, that the Lord Jesus continued, "You are in My way [an offense and a hindrance and a snare to Me]; for you are minding what partakes not of the nature and quality of God, but of men" (16:23, AMP). Of men, that is, who were "sold under sin" (Rom. 7:14), "for the story and message of the cross is sheer absurdity and folly to those who are perishing and on their way to perdition. . . . We are setting these truths forth in words not taught by human wisdom but taught by the [Holy] Spirit, combining and interpreting spiritual truths with spiritual language [to those who possess the Holy Spirit]" (1 Cor. 1:18; 2:13, AMP).

As godliness is the direct and exclusive consequence of God's activity and God's capacity to reproduce Himself in you, so all ungodliness is the direct and exclusive consequence of Satan's activity and of his capacity to reproduce the devil in you!

This is the "mystery of iniquity"! For iniquity is no more the consequence of your capacity to imitate the devil than godliness is the consequence of your capacity to imitate God!

> I know that nothing good dwells within me, that is, in my flesh. I can will what is right, but I cannot perform it. [I have the intention and urge to do what is right, but no power to carry it out.] For I fail to practice the good deeds I desire to do, but the evil deeds that I do not desire

to do are what I am [ever] doing. Now if I do what I do
not desire to do, it is no longer I doing it [it is not myself
that acts], but the sin [principle] which dwells within
me [fixed and operating in my soul]. (Rom. 7:18–20, AMP)

It is a frightening experience to discover what really happens when you commit sin. You cannot, however, begin to
understand the mystery of godliness without beginning to
understand the mystery of iniquity, because the principles involved are identical! When you act in obedience to the truth,
the truth behaves, producing godliness; when you act in obedience to the lie, the lie behaves, producing iniquity!

The Lord Jesus Christ said, "I am . . . the truth" (John 14:6).
All that He was, all that He did and all that He said was God
speaking; He was the Word, and what He communicated
was truth—the truth about God! To see Him was to see the
Father. He was the image of the Invisible because as man He
always obeyed the Spirit of truth, and the Father behaved by
the Spirit through the Son!

If you listen to what God has to say through the Son, you
too will know the truth, for He said, "If you abide in My Word
[hold fast to My teachings and live in accordance with them],
you are truly My disciples. And you will know the Truth, and
the Truth will set you free" (8:31–32, AMP). You will be godly!
The truth will behave—that is to say, the Son will behave by
the Spirit through you, and "if the Son sets you free, you will
be free indeed" (8:36).

Consider now, however, what the Lord Jesus Christ had
to say to the Pharisees:

You are of your father the devil, and your will is to do your
father's desires. He was a murderer from the beginning,
and does not stand in the truth, because there is no truth

in him. When he lies, he speaks out of his own character,
for he is a liar and the father of lies. But because I tell the
truth, you do not believe me. (John 8:44–45)

In other words, as God is the author of truth, so the devil
is the author of deception. The devil is the big lie! Everything
he is, everything he does and everything he says is deceit!

Imagine for one moment that I steal the uniform of a policeman, step out into the middle of a busy street and hold up
my hand. What is the result? All the traffic stops! Although
I am exercising a stolen authority, all the drivers obey me for
the policeman they believe me to be. But what I am is a lie!
They obey my signal—but what I do is a lie! All that I am
and all that I do is one big lie, but the traffic still stops, and I
control the behavior of every driver who does not know the
truth. Everything I say as a bogus policeman will carry the
weight of an authority I do not possess in those who are still
in the dark about the truth and who go on believing a lie.

This—precisely this—is the devil's business. And men
are his merchandise! "The god of this world has blinded the
unbelievers' minds [that they should not discern the truth],
preventing them from seeing the illuminating light of the
Gospel of the glory of Christ, the Messiah, Who is the image
and likeness of God" (2 Cor. 4:4, AMP). And although there
is no truth in him, and all that he is and says and does is a
lie, so long as men walk in darkness and reject the truth as
it has been "embodied and personified" in Jesus Christ (Eph.
4:21, AMP), the devil will go on deceiving them, controlling
their behavior and producing iniquity. They will continue
to do what he says—and the big lie will continue to behave
through them! "Your will is to do your father's desires" (John
8:44).

Iniquity is the inevitable consequence, no matter what you may be doing, if you are acting in obedience to the big lie operating in your soul through the subtle agency of the flesh. Peter was sublimely ignorant of this wicked process, and what he said was quite sincere, but his sincerity did not make it any less iniquitous. He was the mouthpiece of the devil, and what he said was loaded with mischief—and Christ rebuked the devil in the man!

You must be careful not to fall into the same trap. It is pathetically possible to be engaged in all kinds of religious activity that is nothing less than Satan's subtle substitute for salvation. He will pose as "an angel of light" and appeal to your nobler sentiments, and his ministers also will "disguise themselves as servants of righteousness. Their end will correspond to their deeds" (2 Cor. 11:14-15). "Such men are false apostles, deceitful workmen, disguising themselves as apostles of Christ" (11:13). "By smooth talk and flattery they deceive the hearts of the naive" (Rom. 16:18), and "with false words" they "exploit you" (2 Pet. 2:3).

If you are deceived in this way, the end result for you, as it was for the Jews, will be "a zeal for God, but not according to knowledge" (Rom. 10:2)—that is to say, a zeal based in ignorance! What was the nature of their ignorance? They did not know the truth about God's righteousness! They had never entered into the mystery of godliness. They did not know that godliness is the consequence of God's activity in man, so "being ignorant of the righteousness of God," they went about "to establish their own" and did not submit themselves "to God's righteousness" (10:3). Of course, when you go about to establish your own righteousness, all you produce is self-righteousness—your own generous estimate of the measure in which you have conformed, by your own ability, to the object of your own imitation. Any credit that is due, of course, is due to you and you alone. You are to be congratulated!

Is God impressed?

> Not everyone who says to me, "Lord, Lord," will enter the kingdom of heaven, but the one who does the will of my Father who is in heaven. On that day many will say to me, "Lord, Lord, did we not prophesy in your name, and cast out demons in your name, and do many mighty works in your name?" And then will I declare to them, "I never knew you: depart from me, you workers of lawlessness." (Matt. 7:21–23)

In the very name of God and in the practice of religion, you can "work lawlessness!" This is the mystery of iniquity! It is a perpetuation of the Adamic response to the wiles of the devil. The fall of man began with an *act of unbelief*: what Adam *did* when he disobeyed God in the garden was the result of what he *did not believe*, but what he *did not believe* was the result of what he *did believe!*

He did not believe the truth because he did believe a lie, and the lie that he believed was that he could be independent of God with impunity. God had said, "Lose Me, and lose everything—you will die!" and the devil said, "Lose God and lose nothing—you will not die!" What God said was the truth, and what the devil said was a lie about the truth. Every lie is a lie about the truth. The truth is constant; it never changes. Once you have told the truth, the whole truth, and nothing but the truth, you have said everything there is to say—there is nothing more to be said! There is absolutely no limit, however, to the variety of lies that can be told about the truth. But the truth exposes every lie for the lie it is. There is no neutrality in this war! What is not truth is a lie about the truth—and is the enemy of truth!

Adam believed the devil's lie about the truth and thus had no alternative but to reject the truth and behave the lie. Because the lie he believed was that he could be independent of God, the lie he behaved was an act of independence from God—he ate of the forbidden fruit! This was his act of unbelief in relation to the truth, perpetuated by an attitude of unbelief in relation to the truth—an attitude of independence! This attitude is the very essence of sin—of what we have seen is called in the Bible the flesh—and from it stem all the acts that we call sins. Sin is the cause, and sins are the effect; sin is the dirty well, sins are the dirty water!

> From within, out of men's hearts, their evil purposes proceed—fornication, theft, murder, adultery, covetousness, wickedness, deceit, licentiousness, envy, reviling, pride, reckless folly: all these wicked things come out from within and make a man unclean. (Mark 7:21–23, WEY)

It is, however, possible to keep the dirty water inside the dirty well, but this does not make the well clean. Self-interest may produce a hundred and one good reasons for curbing the acts of the flesh without making one iota of difference to its attitude. It will remain as arrogant and proud and hostile to the truth as ever before while presenting a virtuous front to the world around, all dandied up with pious platitudes!

The flesh has an incredible capacity for self-deception, for it derives its nature from the father of lies. At one moment it will advertise its independence from God and hostility to the truth by cursing and swearing, and the next moment will give a pious demonstration of its own self-righteousness by curbing this, its own wicked habit—like a man who stops beating his wife to show her how kind he is!

That is why God says, "The heart is deceitful above all things, and desperately sick; who can understand it?" (Jer. 17:9). No matter how strenuously we may seek to be godly without letting God be the source of our godliness, "we have all become like one who is unclean, and all our righteous deeds are like a polluted garment. We all fade like a leaf, and our iniquities, like the wind, take us away" (Isa. 64:6).

Perhaps I can clarify the issues still further by the use of a simple illustration. Let the human spirit represent the royal residence, prepared by God for the royal Resident, the Holy Spirit. Imagine next that the soul represents the music room, and in it there is the grand piano of human personality—mind, emotion and will. The body, as the amplifier, will communicate the music from the music room to the world around.

Do you get the picture? When God created Adam in his innocency, the Holy Spirit—as the royal Resident imparting the life of God—was at home in Adam's human spirit, the royal residence (top of circle, figure A). He had unchallenged and exclusive access to Adam's soul, the music room (center circle, figure A), and He alone had the right to sit, as it were, at the keyboard of human personality, the grand piano.

Instructing the mind, controlling the emotions and directing the will, the Spirit of truth struck every chord in perfect harmony with the heart of God in heaven, and a matchless melody rang out in evidence that God was reigning in the heart of man on earth!

God, however, had given to man the key to the music room—that is to say, to his soul, or heart—and this key gave man the right to choose out of a free will.

God would not outstay His welcome! The presence of the royal Resident in the royal residence was to be a matter for mutual consent, for there was to be a faith-love relationship between man and God. So long as the music room remained unlocked, offering to the Holy Spirit unchallenged and exclusive access to the keyboard of human personality, God promised that the royal Resident would remain within the royal residence—the Spirit of God within the human spirit—and man would share the very life of God Himself and declare Him to the world in which he lived. At the same time, God made it very clear to man that should the door be locked and access to the music room denied to the royal Resident, He would not remain within the royal residence, and the human spirit would become destitute of the Holy Spirit. In that day man would cease to share the life of God—spiritually he would die!

Man continued to enjoy unbroken fellowship with God until one day the deceiver came—the archenemy of God and destroyer of man's soul, whose name was Lucifer, son of the morning (see Isa. 14:12, KJV). He had rebelled against the truth and become the lie and the father of lies—for there was no more truth in him! More commonly he is known as the devil, or Satan, but he cannot always be readily identified, for often he masquerades as an angel of light.

This deceiver persuaded the first man Adam that man could play the grand piano of human personality without God—and just as well as God! He pointed out the great advantages of being free from the restrictive presence of the Holy Spirit, whose absence, far from detracting from human experience, would undoubtedly enhance it, for man would then be able to pick and choose his own tunes—tunes that needed only to be in harmony with himself and certainly not in harmony with God! Far from losing life by losing God, man would gain life in an entirely new dimension, enjoying things that tasted even better than they looked and that would make him wise—as wise as God! Indeed, man would become his own god, and what could be better than that?

Suffice it to say that the first man Adam believed the lie and locked the door of the music room, and the royal Resident left the royal residence, which became strangely cold and empty. And although he could not quite explain it, Adam had a new and queer sensation that he had never known before. For the want of a better name, he called it fear, and it has never left man since; it still has the same strange effect on him that it had on Adam then. It always makes man want to hide or run away. The funny thing is this: again and again he finds that what has made him run away from God has traveled with him—it is a bad conscience! However, at least Adam was on his own now and could have a crack at that grand piano. What he did not know, however, was that while he had been talking to the lie (that deceiver called Satan), one of the lie's sons (for he is the father of lies) had slipped into the music room!

Later, when Adam looked into the music room, there he was, sitting at the keyboard thumping away at the notes and producing the most excruciating noises, all out of harmony with each other and with everyone else! His name was "the flesh"—and man has never been able to get him away from the grand piano since. At least, not on his own!

It was still the same grand piano, that is to say, the same human personality, but having once produced harmony, it now only produced discord. Adam started quarreling with

Eve and said it was all her fault, but she blamed the devil—
and she wasn't far wrong! Then it spread to the children, and
Cain murdered Abel—and the whole miserable story has
been going on ever since.

No, this is not an extract from *Alice in Wonderland*—I have
been telling you the story of your heart and mine! The Holy
Spirit at the keyboard is the source of all godliness, and the
flesh at the keyboard is the source of all iniquity. You do not
need a new piano—you need a new pianist! That is what the
gospel is all about—how to get the wrong man out and the
right Man in—and to exchange the lie for the truth.

On your own you cannot do it! But I have good news for you.
You can't—*but He* can!

8

The Second Man—
the Lord from Heaven

The last Adam became a life-giving spirit....
The second man is from heaven.
1 Corinthians 15:45, 47

The first man was Adam, and he died; the last Adam is Christ, who came to raise the dead. The first man was of the earth, earthy; the second man is the Lord from heaven. The first is the one who made the mess, and the second is the One who came to clear it up!

In the preceding chapters I trust that you have come more fully to understand what happened when Adam fell and what the inevitable consequences were for him and for the whole race of fallen men. Deprived of the life of God, the animal part of man no longer bore the image of deity, for although "when God created man, he made him *in the likeness of God*," we read that "when Adam had lived 130 years, he fathered a son *in his own likeness*" (Gen. 5:1, 3). Children were born but not in the likeness of God (godlike); they were born in the likeness of their fallen forebearer to carry the marred image of behavior

105

patterns dominated by the flesh throughout all generations. Each child born into the world since the first man Adam died spiritually and ceased to be true man has been born "in Adam," and the consequence of being born "in Adam" is threefold—if nothing happens to change it!

In Adam you are "alienated from the life of God" (Eph.4:18). There is no exception to this rule. And it is not something that will happen, it is something that has already happened! As one who himself had forfeited the life of God, it was utterly impossible for Adam by the physical process of reproduction to impart anything of the divine nature to his offspring. All who have been born in physically alive, soulishly active but spiritually dead Adam, in all succeeding generations, have been born "dead in the trespasses and sins" and have been "by nature children of wrath" (2:1, 3).

In Adam you "walk after the flesh" (see Rom. 8:1; Eph. 2:2–3). There is no exception to this rule! "The LORD looks down from heaven on the children of man, to see if there are any who understand, who seek after God. They have all turned aside; together they have become corrupt: there is none who does good, not even one" (Ps. 14:2–3; see also Rom. 3:10–12). Men are sinners not because they commit sins; men commit sins because by nature they are sinners: "By the one man's disobedience the many were made sinners" (Rom. 5:19). And you were born, as I was, with the wrong man at the grand piano! "You were alienated from God and were enemies in your minds because of your evil behavior" (Col. 1:21, NIV).

In Adam you will "die in your sins" (John 8:24). This is the third and final consequence of being "in Adam": at the time of physical death, if nothing happens to change the situation between your physical birth and your physical death, you will die in the condition in which you were born—spiritually dead—but your soul will survive to be held morally responsible to God for a wasted life and to "pay the penalty and suffer the punishment of everlasting ruin (destruction and perdition) and eternal exclusion and banishment from the presence of the Lord and from the glory of His power" (2 Thess. 1:9, AMP). And there is certainly no exception to this rule!

The Virgin Birth of Jesus Christ Presupposes the Utter Depravity of Man

Had God not intervened, there never could have been a "*second man*" to walk this earth as God intended man to be. That is why the *virgin birth* of Jesus Christ is not a matter of secondary importance—it is *imperative*.

Had Jesus Christ been born as you and I were born, by natural conception, He too would have been "in Adam," spiritually dead, uninhabited by God and dominated only by the flesh with its roots in the devil—condemned already to die physically as He had been born physically: cut off from God. As a sinner by nature, He would have been a sinner in practice, a fallen member of the fallen race of fallen men.

You cannot reject the virgin birth of Jesus Christ without repudiating His deity and His sinlessness—unless you are prepared to repudiate the fall of man! For fallen man does not have what it takes to be sinless. He is spiritually bankrupt and without God—and it takes God to make a man godly!

To insist that Jesus Christ came into this world by natural birth and lived a sinless life is to repudiate the fall of man! It means that what was possible to Him as a natural man must be possible to you and to me as natural men, so that if we are not what He was, it is only because we do not try hard enough!

If this were true, the message of the gospel would simply be an exhortation to greater effort—an attempt to realize the inherent adequacy that is self-existent within every human being—including Christ! A message of spiritual regeneration would become patently superfluous and the fall of man a myth, for by nature man would have what it takes to live uprightly!

This in fact would mean that man can master his own grand piano and emancipate himself, conquering his own soul! Pardon me, but if I am not mistaken, I think I just saw the big lie smiling around the corner! Someone has just made him a doctor of divinity!

A theological student came to me not long ago and said that he had just listened to his first lecture on Luke's Gospel. The learned professor had announced his subject as "The Virgin Birth of Jesus Christ—*Neither True nor Necessary*"! To be as ignorant as that of the basic essentials of the truth would be tragic enough in the simple minded, but to expose such ignorance in the name of scholarship to a class of students is criminal negligence and a masterpiece of satanic genius of which only the devil himself could be capable.

To *accept* the fall of man and still insist upon the natural birth of Christ is to number the Lord at once with sinful men, for "all have sinned and fall short of the glory of God" (Rom. 3:23), and "the Scripture imprisoned everything under sin" (Gal. 3:22). John is speaking of the whole race of man when he says in his epistle, "If we say we have no sin, we deceive ourselves, and the truth is not in us. . . . If we say we have not sinned, we make him [God] a liar, and his word is not in us" (1 John 1:8, 10). If Christ had been born naturally, He would have been no exception to the rule of those who "in Adam" walk after the flesh and thus inevitably sin.

Robbed of His deity and robbed of His sinlessness, what would be left of His work of redemption? His vicarious sufferings on the cross would be stripped of all validity, for He could only have suffered for His own sins but never for the sins of others. His glorious act of atonement would be reduced to an empty, sentimental gesture, the tragic end of a noble idealist who drifted to disaster because He lived before His time. His resurrection would be totally unnecessary and, to avoid embarrassment, must be explained away as the wishful thinking of some hysterical women or the ingenious invention of some of His over-enthusiastic disciples!

Deny the virgin birth of Jesus Christ, and you have laid the axe to all the essential doctrines of the Bible: the fall and depravity of man, the deity and sinlessness of Christ, the atoning efficacy of His death and resurrection, the necessity for spiritual regeneration as the basis for holiness of life and the truth of the Bible itself! Little wonder that those who deny the virgin birth of Christ have little love for the Word of God, for the truth exposes every lie for the lie it is, and every lie is a lie about the truth!

The Virgin Birth of Jesus Christ Furnishes the First Requirement for Man's Redemption: A Sinless Sacrifice

As descendants of the first Adam, we were born uninhabited by God—heirs of His absence—and inhabited only by sin. The Lord Jesus Christ, miraculously conceived by the Holy Spirit in the womb of Mary, was born uninhabited by sin and wholly inhabited by God! He was the last Adam—the second man—as sinless as He Himself had created man to be. He was able to turn to His disciples and say, "The ruler of this world [the devil] is coming. He has no claim on me" (John 14:30).

Look again at the diagram on page 77 and consider figure C. This represents the Lord Jesus Christ as He was on earth: never less than God but always completely man! He, though tempted in all points as we are, was without sin. Though of all other men the Father could only say, "None is righteous, no, not one" (Rom. 3:10), of this, the second man, the Father could say, "This is my beloved Son, with whom I am well pleased" (Matt. 17:5). He was the first requirement for man's redemption—a sinless sacrifice and substitute:

> In Christ God was reconciling the world to himself, not counting their trespasses against them, and entrusting to us the message of reconciliation. . . . For our sake he made him to be sin who knew no sin, so that in him we might become the righteousness of God. (2 Cor. 5:19, 21)

How did the Lord Jesus Christ in His perfect manhood present Himself to the Father? Through the Holy Spirit (represented in figure C by the smaller lined circle within the human spirit of Christ as man): "Christ . . . through the eternal Spirit offered himself without blemish to God" (Heb. 9:14). Because of this, the life of God, once clothed on earth with the humanity of the first man Adam in his innocency (figure A), then forfeited by the first man Adam in his depravity (figure B), is now clothed again on earth with the spotless humanity of the second man, Christ—the Lord from heaven (figure C), the last Adam, the quickening Spirit. And He restores the dead to life!

You will notice that in figure C there is no smaller circle placed within the center circle representing the soul of the Lord Jesus Christ, for as perfect man He placed His total personality at the Father's disposal—the prince of this world, the devil, had nothing in Him. The result was that for the first time since Adam fell into sin, there was the perfect image of the invisible God in bodily form on earth: "He is the exact likeness of the unseen God. . . . For in Him the whole fullness of Deity (the Godhead), continues to dwell in bodily form [giving complete expression of the divine nature]" (Col. 1:15; 2:9, AMP).

To indicate the unchanging deity of Christ even in His humanity, the circle C, representing the body of Christ, is patterned, as are both circles that represent Christ's soul and His spirit. The complete expression of the divine nature in all His human behavior is indicated by the gray margin at the circumference of circle C, as this once was true of the first man in his innocency (see circle A).

If God withdrew His life from man when sin came in, under what circumstances will God restore His life to man? Only when sin has been cleansed and forgiven. The Lord Jesus said, "I have come that they may have life, and have it to the full" (John 10:10, NIV). He did not come that men might have physical life—they had that. He came that men might have spiritual life—restoring the dead to life!

As the first requirement for man's redemption—a sinless sacrifice—the Lord Jesus gave Himself upon the cross and "suffered once for sins, the righteous for the unrighteous, that he might bring us to God" (1 Pet. 3:18). "The blood of Jesus his Son cleanses us from all sin" (1 John 1:7). But it is essential that you should realize that His cross was the means to an end; for to confuse the means for the end is to rob the Lord Jesus of that for which He came.

He came that you might have life! His *life*! *His life*—imparted to you by the renewing of the Holy Spirit on the grounds of redemption, to reinhabit your spirit, to reconquer your soul, so that you might be "transfigured into His very own image in ever increasing splendor and from one degree of glory to another; [for this comes] from the Lord [Who is] the Spirit" (2 Cor. 3:18, AMP). He came to restore to you all that makes the mystery of godliness an open secret—the presence of the living God within a human soul.

This is the way from death to life!

When the Holy Spirit convicts you of the fact that you are a sinner and spiritually dead—"in Adam" and at enmity with God—and you repent and turn to Christ, humbly accepting Him as your Savior and welcoming Him back by His Holy Spirit to live within you and to take control of you, this is your conversion!

In point of fact, it is a reconversion. As the first man Adam was once converted—changing his mind about God at the place of first choice, the tree in the garden—so you, the heir by nature of his Adamic attitude of independence, change your mind about his change of mind at the place of second choice, the tree on the hill—the cross!

Adam was created knowing the truth from within, through the Spirit, and he listened to the lie from without, through the word of Satan. He exchanged the truth of God for a lie—the truth went out, and the lie came in. He stepped out of dependence into independence—out of life into death! You were born blinded by the lie from within through the flesh, and you listen to the truth from without through the Word of God. When you repent, you accept the truth and obey it, stepping back out of independence into dependence—out of death into life! "Truly, truly, I say to you, whoever hears my word and believes him who sent me has everlasting life. He does not come into judgment, but has passed from death to life" (John 5:24).

The moment you repent and obey the truth in genuine conversion, God accepts you for Christ's sake as a forgiven sinner, for "he himself bore our sins in his body on the tree" (1 Pet. 2:24). Judgment has already been executed on your sin vicariously in the person of the sinless Substitute, and you are acquitted. This is called redemption.

Conversion is man moving Godward, and redemption is God moving manward. God took the initiative, through His incarnation in the virgin birth of Christ, in providing at Calvary the place where sinners may be reconciled to Himself through the atoning sacrifice of His sinless Son. But man must take the initiative in appropriating by faith this salvation that grace has provided. Grace provides, but faith appropriates, so that "it is by grace that you have been saved through faith; and that not of yourselves. It is God's gift, and is not on the ground of merit" (Eph. 2:8–9, WEY).

God bears witness to the faith that appropriates redemption by the gift of the Holy Spirit, and this renewing of the Holy Spirit is called regeneration, or new birth. "God, who knows all hearts, gave His testimony in their favour by bestowing the Holy Spirit on them just as He did on us; and He made no difference between us and them, in that He cleansed their hearts by their faith" (Acts 15:8–9, WEY). The gift of the Holy Spirit to those who believe is the end toward which the cross was but the means. Redemption was never designed by God simply to make you fit for heaven—it was designed to clear the decks for spiritual regeneration, which would make you fit for earth on the way to heaven! You cannot be spiritually regenerate without first being redeemed, but you cannot be redeemed without becoming, in consequence, spiritually regenerate. It is the latter that adds validity to the former and is the seal of your faith:

> In Him you Gentiles also, after listening to the Message of the truth, the Good News of your salvation—having believed in Him—were sealed with the promised Holy Spirit; that Spirit being a pledge and foretaste of our inheritance, in anticipation of its full redemption. (Eph. 1:13–14, WEY)

It had always been God's plan to abolish death and bring "life and immortality to light" by the "appearing of our Savior Jesus Christ" (2 Tim. 1:10). Speaking to "that ancient serpent, who is called the devil and Satan, the deceiver of the whole world" (Rev. 12:9), God had said, "I will put enmity between you and the woman, and between your offspring and her offspring; he shall bruise your head, and you shall bruise his heel" (Gen. 3:15). This offspring, or "seed"—the seed of the woman (Mary)—was the seed promised by God to faithful Abraham: "In your offspring [seed] shall all the nations of the earth be blessed" (22:18). Miraculously conceived and born at Bethlehem, the second man, the Lord from heaven, Christ, "redeemed us from the curse of the law by becoming a curse for us—for it is written, 'Cursed is everyone who is hanged on a tree'—so that in Christ Jesus the blessing of Abraham might come to the Gentiles, so that we might receive the promised Spirit through faith" (Gal. 3:13–14).

Thus the promise inherent in God's word to Abraham was the renewing of the Holy Spirit—spiritual regeneration—the raising of the dead!

The Virgin Birth of Jesus Christ Establishes a Precedent in Procedure for Spiritual Regeneration

What were the events that led up to the birth of Christ? How did it all begin, so far as Mary was concerned?

It began with the word—a message of truth faithfully delivered by the angel Gabriel, who "was sent from God" (Luke 1:26). The truth that the angel communicated was at once strange and startling, contrary to all human experience and beyond natural explanation: "You have found favor with God. And behold, you will conceive in your womb and bear a son, and you shall call his name Jesus. He will be great and will be called the Son of the Most High. . . . Of his kingdom there will be no end" (1:30–33).

The natural reaction of the natural heart of this natural woman was one of incredulity! The obvious question to be asked and answered was "How?" So Mary said to the angel, "How can this be . . . seeing that I have no husband?" (1:34, WEY). She deliberately denied the prerequisite for natural birth, and Joseph too denied any responsibility for parenthood!

> The circumstances of the birth of Jesus Christ were these. After his mother Mary was betrothed to Joseph, before they were united in marriage, she was found to be with child through the Holy Spirit. But Joseph her husband, being a kind-hearted man and unwilling publicly to disgrace her, had determined to release her privately from the betrothal. (Matt. 1:18–19, WEY)

The facts of the case then are quite clear: Mary denied intimacy with any man, and Joseph repudiated responsibility for the birth of Christ so emphatically that he was about to break his engagement with Mary for her supposed infidelity.

Those who would have you reject the virgin birth of Christ, therefore, would have you believe that He was the illegitimate child of a woman who was both unfaithful and a liar! Others would have you believe that a matter of such gravity is of no particular consequence. Remember that every lie is a lie about the truth—and every lie comes from the same source, the big lie, who is the father of lies.

> As [Joseph] was thinking this over, behold, an angel of the Lord appeared to him in a dream, saying, Joseph, descendant of David, do not be afraid to take Mary [as] your wife, for that which is conceived in her is of (from, out of) the Holy Spirit. She will bear a Son, and you shall call His name Jesus [the Greek form of the Hebrew Joshua, which means Savior], for He will save His people from their sins [that is, prevent them from failing and missing the true end and scope of life, which is God]. (Matt. 1:20–21, AMP)

Joseph too received the word of truth and believed it, a message from God in confirmation of the prophecy of Isaiah: "The LORD called me from the womb, from the body of my mother he named my name" (49:1). Christ was announced and named a boy, Jesus—before He was born! Maybe you have never thought of this—for we take so much for granted—but supposing Mary had had a baby girl!

"Mary," the angel might have said, "you ask 'How?' But there is no human explanation! Yet I will tell you how:

> "The Holy Spirit will come upon you, and the power of the Most High will overshadow you [like a shining cloud]; and so the holy (pure, sinless) Thing (Offspring) which shall be born of you will be called the Son of God." (Luke 1:35, AMP)

How was it to be?

By the word of God, through the Holy Spirit! All the mighty power of God to implement the word of God to clothe the life of God with man's humanity was made available through the Holy Spirit. But was this enough? No! One condition still needed to be met: Mary's availability to this gracious, life-begetting ministry of the Holy Spirit.

Maybe you tend to take for granted the fact that Mary should place herself at God's disposal! Is there any reason why you should assume this? Have you placed yourself completely at God's disposal? Is there any reason why you should expect of her what you are not prepared to do yourself? Mary might have said, "I do not want God to interfere in my life! I am engaged to be married, and I have my own plans! This is going to spoil everything!" Isn't this what you have often said or thought? In any case, who was going to believe her story?

Who did believe Mary's story? When the Pharisees said to the Lord Jesus Christ, "We are not illegitimate children and born out of fornication; we have one Father, even God" (John 8:41, AMP), it was a sly, stinging, wicked reference to the birth of the Savior, by which these "serpents" and this "brood of vipers" (Matt. 23:33) identified themselves with those godless theologians of all generations who have denied and still deny the virgin birth of Christ! Of these Christ would say today, as He said of the Pharisees then, "You are of your father the devil" (John 8:44).

In the light of events and in retrospect, it is easy for us to call her blessed, but for Mary then it was the *deliberate obedience of faith*. By it she died to all her own plans, to all her own reputation and to all those hopes that had been fixed in the one whom she had loved most dearly! "Mary said, 'Behold, I am the servant of the Lord; let it be to me according to your word'" (Luke 1:38). From that moment on, the onus was on God to fulfill the promise He had made and to do what He had said!

By the word of God, through the Holy Spirit, acting on the obedience of faith. That is how the miracle took place, and Christ was born at Bethlehem—the second man, the Lord from heaven!

As utter God and perfect man, by His incarnation the Lord Jesus Christ had established a precedent in procedure for spiritual regeneration. The words of the Lord Jesus Christ to Nicodemus were as startling and strange as those of the angel Gabriel to Mary—"Truly, truly, I say to you, unless one is born again he cannot see the kingdom of God" (John 3:3)— and the natural reaction of the natural heart of this natural man to these unnatural words was one of equal incredulity! The obvious question to be asked and answered was "How?" Nicodemus said to the Lord, "How can a man be born when he is old? Can he enter a second time into his mother's womb and be born?" (3:4).

"You want to know how, Nicodemus?" the Lord Jesus might have said. "There is no human explanation! Yet I will tell you how:" "The wind blows where it wishes, and you hear its sound, but you do not know where it comes from or where it goes. So it is with everyone who is born of the Spirit" (3:8). "That is how, Nicodemus—by the Holy Spirit!" By the word of God (from the lips of Christ Himself!) and through the Holy Spirit. By his very question, though one of the noblest of the Pharisees, Nicodemus exposed the fact that he only knew of one quality of life—that which he had received by his natural, animal birth from his natural, animal parents. But "God is spirit, and those who worship him must worship in spirit and truth" (John 4:24). So the Lord Jesus Christ had to explain to him, "That which is born of the flesh is flesh" (3:6)—and "flesh and blood" no more inherit the kingdom of God than "does the perishable inherit the imperishable" (1 Cor. 15:50)!

"That which is born of the Spirit is spirit" (John 3:6), and if there is nothing "born of the Spirit" in that which is "born of the flesh," then that which is "born of the flesh" is spiritually bankrupt. If you are still in this condition, you need to be born again, and all the mighty power of God to implement the word of God and so to clothe the life of God with you has been made available through the Holy Spirit!

Is it enough, however, that the Holy Spirit is both able and willing to give to you "all things that pertain to life and godliness" and to make you a partaker "of the divine nature" (2 Pet. 1:3–4)? No! You too must yield the obedience of faith! Changing your mind about Adam's change of mind about God, you must get back to God by a deliberate act of faith, just as Adam lost Him by a deliberate act of unbelief.

You must look up into God's face and say, "Maybe I do not fully understand how the death of Your dear Son and the precious blood that He shed can cleanse my heart from sin and clear the record—but this is what You have said! Be it unto me according to Your word! Maybe I do not fully understand how You can come by Your Holy Spirit to live in me, making me a partaker of the very life of Jesus Christ Himself so that He through me can reveal the invisible God to a visible world, but this is what You have said! Be it unto me, oh God! Be it unto me according to Your word!"

Do that, and the onus is on God to keep the promise He has made and to do what He has said! You *can't*—but He *can*!

The Virgin Birth of Jesus Christ Demonstrates the Principle of an Imparted Life

Joseph and Mary were accustomed each year to go to Jerusalem at the feast of the Passover, and on one of these occasions, when the Lord Jesus Christ was just twelve years old, they were returning home. "Supposing him to be in the group they went a day's journey" (Luke 2:44). Having missed Him, however, they went back to Jerusalem to find Him three days later in the temple, "sitting among the teachers, listening to them and asking them questions" (2:46).

When Joseph and Mary saw the "little Lord Jesus," "they were amazed; and His mother said to Him, Child, why have You treated us like this? Here Your father and I have been anxiously looking for You [distressed and tormented]" (2:48, AMP). Jesus asked them a very pointed question: "How is it that you had to look for Me?" (2:49, AMP). In other words, "Why did you suppose that I was in the group? Don't you know that I am wholly, exclusively available to My Father; that My whole humanity is at His disposal and I must always be about His business and doing the things that please Him? Why should you suppose that where you want to go is where I want to go? It all depends whether where you want to go is in My Father's interests."

By the miraculous birth of the Lord Jesus Christ, conceived of the Holy Spirit, the Father clothed Himself with the sinless humanity of the Son in that body that He had "prepared" (Heb. 10:5) for Him in the womb of Mary, and the Son presented Himself without spot to the Father so that He could say, "The Father who dwells in me does his works" (John 14:10).

Through His obedience as the second man and the last

Adam, the Lord Jesus became a "life-giving Spirit" (1 Cor. 15:45, AMP), able to cleanse you from sin through His atoning death and restore you to life by His indwelling Spirit, that He might live in and through you as the Father lived in and through Him. Why then do you "suppose" that He is "in the group"—that where you want to go and what you want to do is always where He wants to go? Don't you know that the Lord Jesus Christ lives in you to be about His Father's business and to do what He wants to do?

"And [Jesus] went down with [Joseph and Mary] and came to Nazareth and was submissive to them" (Luke 2:51). Having established the principle quite clearly at this early age of twelve, both to Joseph and to Mary, that He was irrevocably committed to His Father, the amazing thing is that Jesus then "was submissive to them." In other words, He would go where they went and do what they did, but "His mother carefully treasured up all these incidents in her memory" (2:51, WEY), and she knew from then on that wherever she asked Him to go and whatever she asked Him to do, she first had to ask her own heart, "Am I committed to Him for all that to which He is committed to His Father?"

Are you committed to Christ without question and without complaint for all that to which He in you is committed to the Father? This is the principle of His imparted life! It involves complete, deliberate abandonment to Christ in everything.

> Do you not know that your body is the temple [the very sanctuary] of the Holy Spirit Who lives within you, Whom you have received [as a Gift] from God? You are not your own, you were bought with a price [purchased with a preciousness and paid for, made His own]. So

then, honor God and bring glory to Him in your body. (1 Cor. 6:19–20, AMP)

There came a day, at the marriage feast in Cana of Galilee, when Mary learned to say, "Do whatever he tells you" (John 2:5). She had learned that He was not subject to her but that she was subject to Him, and that was at the beginning of Jesus' public ministry!

When you have learned that He is not subject to you but that you are subject to Him, that will be the beginning of His public ministry in you. You will "be constantly renewed in the spirit of your mind [having a fresh mental and spiritual attitude]," and you will "put on the new nature (the regenerate self) created in God's image, [Godlike] in true righteousness and holiness" (Eph. 4:23–24, AMP). And the second man, the Lord from heaven, will reveal Himself again to a needy world through you.

The wrong man will be *out*—and the right Man will be *in*!

9

The Law of the Spirit of Life

The law of the Spirit of life has set you free in Christ Jesus
from the law of sin and death.
Romans 8:2

The Spirit and life are as inseparable as sin and death, and there can be no more compromise between the Spirit and sin than there is between life and death—each is diametrically opposed to the other. That is why to be "in Christ" instead of "in Adam" involves a radical change of government. It introduces a new law!

It was to bring about this change of government and introduce this new law that the second man was born at Bethlehem, lived, died and rose again from the dead: "For as by the one man's disobedience the many were made sinners, so by the one man's obedience the many will be made righteous" (Rom. 5:19). The total availability of the Lord Jesus Christ to the Father—to be "about His business"—was such that "after He had appeared in human form, He abased and humbled Himself [still further] and carried His obedience to the extreme of death, even the death of the cross" (Phil. 2:8, AMP). And, as we have already seen, obedience is the criterion of faith!

As the last Adam, the Lord Jesus Christ was the antithesis of the first Adam. Adam died by faith because he obeyed the lie; Christ lived by faith because He obeyed the truth. That is to say, He was so subject to the "law of the Spirit of life" that His total personality "declared" the Father:

> No man has ever seen God at any time; the only unique Son, or the only begotten God, Who is in the Bosom [in the intimate presence] of the Father, He has declared him [He has revealed Him and brought Him out where He can be seen; He has interpreted Him and He has made Him known]. (John 1:18, AMP)

It is this law, however, operating "in Christ Jesus" that, the apostle Paul writes, "has set [you] free . . . from the law of sin and death" (Rom. 8:2). How can a law that operated in Him liberate you and me? This is the question that I want to explore with you in this chapter.

What the Law Could Not Do

Do not confuse the law with the law of the Spirit of life nor with the law of sin and death. This is the Old Testament law, and contained within it, of course, are the Ten Commandments. It is the law of righteousness. What then could this law not do?

The law "made nothing perfect" (Heb. 7:19). The reason for this is now self-evident, for although the demands of the law are strong and uncompromising, the law is "weakened by the flesh [the entire nature of man without the Holy Spirit]" (Rom. 8:3, AMP). As one born uninhabited by God and inhabited only by the flesh, you discover that "the mind of the flesh [with its carnal thoughts and purposes] is hostile to God, for it does not submit itself to God's law; indeed it cannot" (Rom. 8:7, AMP).

God, as it were, wrote the score, but the wrong man at the grand piano refuses to play the tune! He prefers the liberty of improvisation to the discipline of following the music and the thrill of self-willed syncopation to the steady rhythm of a life in tune with God. Every departure from the score is a transgression of the law, and the transgression of the law is sin (1 John 3:4). Has this not been your experience? Written with the "finger of God" (Exod. 31:18), the law represents the minimum demands of God's righteousness, and godliness will no more derive from your attempts to fulfill the law than from your attempts to imitate God—you can do neither! For the law of sin and death within you is hostile both to God and to His law of righteousness, and so the law "made nothing perfect"!

It is a source of untold relief to discover that God has never expected anything of you but unremitting failure. Nothing that ever shocks you about yourself shocks Him—it grieves Him but never shocks Him. You cannot be shocked by what you expect! If you are still shocked at your own capacity for wickedness, it is because you have never fully repented. You still do not believe what God says about you—that you are "of the flesh, sold under sin" and that in you, that is in your "lower self, nothing good has its home" (Rom. 7:14, 18, WEY).

You are still believing the devil's lie about the truth and rejecting God's truth about the devil's lie. You are still committing the sin of Saul, who presumed to spare "the best" and "all that was good" (1 Sam. 15:9) in what God had totally condemned, and the folly of Jehoshaphat, who had false hopes of an unholy covenant, helped the "wicked" and loved "those who hate the LORD" (2 Chron. 19:2; see also 18:3).

You may be "in Christ," but you are behaving as though you were "in Adam"—perpetuating the Adamic creed of self-sufficiency, shocked when you can't only because you insist on believing that you can! You adopt the attitude of the defeated tennis player who says that there must be something wrong with his tennis racket!

I do not mean that God excuses your sin or expects you to go on sinning. I simply mean that He has absolutely no delusions whatever about you for what you are apart from what He is! Why go on having delusions about yourself? Repentance does not simply go on apologizing to God for the things you have done wrong, as though you were surprised at yourself. In that way you only advertise your own conceit, as though you were waiting for God to say, "I know that you did not mean it, and it is not what I would normally expect of you," when it is exactly what you did mean and exactly what God always expects of you! Why not call your own bluff (and the devil's!) and recognize the nature of the beast, for true repentance humbly admits not only that what you have done is wrong but that what you have done is the inevitable consequence of what you are—unless what you are is replaced through the Holy Spirit by what He is!

It is the Holy Spirit who is diametrically opposed to sin, and only His presence introduces the liberating law of life. The flesh loves sin, and in all its most subtle forms, including "our righteous deeds"—the "filthy rags" (Isa. 64:6, KJV) of pseudo-piety and self-advertisement. Stop being deceived into thinking that the flesh will ever change its nature. Its roots are always in the devil! The late Captain Reginald Wallis used to say, "Far too many people have shares in the Old Adam Improvement Society." It has been a bankrupt concern ever since the company was floated, and when the Lord comes, it will go into final liquidation!

The law can no more make you godly than a railway guide can make a train run on time—and by nature you are always behind schedule! There is good news, however—good news for you, no matter how discouraged you may be, for *"God has done what the Law could not do"* (Rom. 8:3, AMP).

How did He do it? "By sending his own Son in the likeness of sinful flesh and for sin, he condemned sin in the flesh, in order that the righteous requirement of the law might be fulfilled in us, who walk not according to the flesh but according to the Spirit" (8:3). God passed judgment upon sin in your very nature in a twofold way: morally and vicariously. He sent His Son in the first place "in the likeness of sinful flesh" to condemn sin morally, and in the second place He sent His Son "for sin" to condemn sin vicariously.

Though "in the likeness of," the Lord Jesus Christ was not sinful as "sinful flesh," for He was without sin, specifically the only begotten Son of God, conceived miraculously of the Holy Spirit in the womb of a virgin: "From the beginning He had the nature of God" (Phil. 2:6, WEY). As opposed to the spiritually bankrupt stock of the first and fallen Adam, who were "ignorant of the righteousness which God provides and building their hopes upon a righteousness of their own," the second and last Adam had the righteousness of God inherently in Him, for "Christ is the termination of Law to every believer" (Rom. 10:3–4, WEY).

Every demand made by the law in righteousness found its complete fulfillment in the person of the Lord Jesus Christ. There was no point at which the law could accuse Him! In the beginning with God and as the law's author (as God), Christ was the law's fulfillment in righteousness. As utter man He satisfied His own demands as utter God, and His utterness was given utterance in utter righteousness! He was the Word through whom God speaks, and what He has to say at first condemns you! It is quite obvious that the righteousness of Christ's life may be equated with the righteousness demanded by God's law. This being so, what can the life He lived then, nineteen hundred years ago, do for you now?

If the life He lived then simply demonstrated the righteousness demanded by the law, then all that His life can do for you now is what the law can do for you now—and we know what the law cannot do: it cannot make you perfect! The law condemns you and proves you guilty:

> We know that whatever the law says it speaks to those who are under the law, so that every mouth may be stopped, and the whole world may be held accountable to God. For by the works of the law no human being will be justified in his sight, since through the law comes knowledge of sin. (Rom. 3:19–20)

Christ's life also condemns you and proves you guilty! Compare your life with the demands that the law makes upon you, and your mouth will be stopped. Your sin will be exposed, and you will be proved guilty! Whether you try to fulfill the law or imitate His life, both will condemn you morally. By two equally absolute standards of measurement, you will be exposed for the sinner you are, for you "fall short of the glory of God" (3:23). The plumb line may show me that the wall in my garden is crooked, but it will not put it straight, and had Jesus Christ come into this world simply to demonstrate a sinless life and leave us with a matchless example, He would have left us to wallow in the squalor of our own inadequacy. The "good news" of the gospel would have been a message of despair—to mock us without being able to mend us!

The life He lived on earth condemns you, for He could—but you can't! Then why did He live a life that can only condemn you now?

The Life He Lived Qualified Him for the Death He Died

The Lord Jesus Christ could not have died the death He died had He not lived the life He lived. He could have suffered a martyr's death, a prophet's death, a preacher's death—the death of a noble idealist, the champion of some lofty cause or the hero of some courageous enterprise destined to bless mankind, but *not a Savior's death!* "Christ [the Messiah Himself] died for sins once for all, the Righteous for the unrighteous (the Just for the unjust, the Innocent for the guilty) that He might bring us to God" (1 Pet. 3:18, AMP).

> Because the sinless Savior died,
> My sinful soul is counted free;
> And God the Just is satisfied,
> To look on Him, and pardon me!

God sent His Son into the world not only "in the likeness of sinful flesh" to condemn sin morally but "for sin" to condemn sin vicariously.

"For our sake he made him to be sin who knew no sin, so that in him we might become the righteousness of God" (2 Cor. 5:21). The Bible leaves us in absolutely no doubt about the significance of the death of Christ: He died in your place and mine, incurring for our sakes a penalty that He did not deserve. This was no sentimental gesture but a deliberate act of redemption!

Apart from His death, His life could only condemn us, like the law that His life fulfilled. But His death added *grace to truth:*

G—God's

R—riches

A—at

C—Christ's

E—expense

Truth declared by the law and fulfilled by His life convicts sinners of their sins and tells them to be sorry, but grace provided by His death tells sinners who are sorry how they may be saved! "The law was given through Moses; grace and truth came through Jesus Christ" (John 1:17).

Without a sinless life, the Lord Jesus Christ could never have suffered a vicarious, substitutionary and atoning death. To deny the supernatural nature of His birth is to deny His deity; to deny His deity is to deny His sinlessness; and to deny His sinlessness is to deny the atonement. And to deny that is to deny that God has done what the law could not do!

Have you accepted Christ as your Redeemer? Do you know that for His dear sake your sins are forgiven? You may know this just as soon as you say, "Thank You, Lord! Be it unto me according to Your Word! Redeem my soul, cleanse my heart and wash me in the blood of the Lamb—the Lamb of God who takes away the sin of the world!"

> In peace let me resign my breath,
> And Thy salvation see;
> My sins deserve eternal death,
> But Jesus died for me!

To know your sins are gone is joy indeed! The record cleansed, you are reconciled to God, heaven is now your home. But is that really all you need?

It is where you must begin, but it is not all you need!

Does the knowledge that your sins have been forgiven in itself impart to you any new capacity to live a different kind of life? The answer obviously is no!

There may have been created within you a genuine desire to serve God out of a sincere sense of gratitude to Christ for dying for you. You may be impelled out of a sense of duty as a Christian to seek conformity to some pattern of behavior that has been imposed upon you as the norm for Christian living. You may be deeply moved by the need of others all around you, and holy ambitions may have been stirred within your heart to count for God. If however, all that has happened is that your sins have been forgiven because you have accepted Christ as the Savior who died for you, leaving you since your conversion only with those resources that you had before your conversion, then you will have no alternative but to Christianize the flesh and try to teach it to behave in such a way that it will be godly!

That is a sheer impossibility! The nature of the flesh never changes, no matter how you may coerce it or conform it. It is rotten through and through, even with a Bible under its arm, a check for missions in its hand and an evangelical look on its face. You need something more than forgiveness—what you need is the big news of the gospel! This is the very heart of the message.

The Death That He Died Qualifies You for the Life That He Lived

The moment you are redeemed through the atoning death of Christ upon the cross, you receive the Holy Spirit within your human spirit. Looking back at the illustration on page 77, this is represented by the small lined circle within the top circle of figure D. You have "passed from death to life"—raised from the dead—and the life that has been imparted to you by the Holy Spirit is the very life of Christ Himself: "He made us alive together in fellowship and in union with Christ; [He gave us the very life of Christ Himself, the same new life with which He quickened Him]" (Eph. 2:5, AMP).

The life that the Lord Jesus Christ lived for you nineteen hundred years ago condemns you, but the life that He now lives in you saves you! The Christian life is the life that He lived then lived now by Him in you. As He behaved in the sinless humanity that the Father had prepared for Him then, so He wants to behave in your humanity presented to Him now. This means your mind placed at His disposal through the indwelling Holy Spirit; your emotions, your will, all that you are and have, made available to the Lord Jesus Christ as a living member of His new corporate body on earth, which is called the church.

This is the new law in action, the law of the Spirit of life in Christ Jesus, reestablishing the faith-love relationship between your soul and God and making it possible for you to "declare" the Son as once the Son "declared" the Father. Your behavior mechanism, once more wholly Deo-centric instead of egocentric "so that the commandment of the law may find fulfillment" in you, is no longer under the control of your lower nature but "is directed by the Spirit." A radical change of government! We see then certain principles evolving, and I would like to summarize them in four simple sentences.

He had to come as He did (by a miraculous birth) to be what He was (perfect). Christ's supernatural birth qualified Him for the sinless life He lived—the Word incarnate, never less than God in what He was but never more than man in what He did! Completely empty of sin, always filled with the Spirit, led by the Spirit and empowered by the Spirit (see Luke 4:1, 14).

Could He not have chosen His own path and made His own decisions? As God, yes! As man, no! Did He have no power of His own? As God, enough to create the universes, throw them into space and keep them there "by the word of his power" (Heb. 1:3)! As man, none! "Jesus said to them, 'Truly, truly, I say to you, the Son can do nothing of his own accord, but only what he sees the Father doing. For whatever the Father does, that the Son does likewise'" (John 5:19).

He had to be what He was (perfect) to do what He did (redeem). Only by virtue of His own sinlessness could Christ die vicariously for those whose sin His life had condemned morally. God has done what the law could not do!

> He knew how wicked man had been,
> He knew that God must punish sin;
> So out of pity Jesus said:
> I'll bear the punishment instead!

He had to do what He did (redeem) that you might have what He is (life). Here is the "much more" of your salvation: Christ in the present tense! Not what He was—that would condemn you. And not just what He will be—that would only tantalize you. But He gives you all the overwhelming adequacy of all that He is right now for every step of the way and for every bend in the road. "For if while we were enemies we were reconciled to God by the death of his Son, much more, now that we are reconciled, shall we be saved by his life" (Rom. 5:10).

You must have what He is (life) to be what He was (perfect). Godliness is not the consequence of your capacity to imitate God but the consequence of His capacity to reproduce Himself in you. It is not self-righteousness but Christ-righteousness, the righteousness that is by faith—a faith that by renewed dependence upon God releases His divine action to restore the marred image of the invisible God. It is not inactivity but Christ-activity—God in action accomplishing the divine end through human personality; never reducing man to the status of a cabbage but exalting man to the stature of a king! "For if, because of one man's trespass, death reigned through that one man, much more will those who receive the abundance of grace and the free gift of righteousness reign in life through the one man Jesus Christ" (5:17).

At first sight this might seem to offer to you the possibility of sinless perfection as the result of spiritual regeneration, but this is far from being the case. For it is only your faith and your obedience that allow Him to be in you now what He was then (perfect), and you will be what He was then only to the degree in which you allow Him to be in you what He is now (perfect)!

All of the Father was available to all of the Son, because by His faith-love relationship all of the Son was available to all of the Father, and this constituted His perfect manhood. And the availability of the Son to you will be in the degree of your availability to the Son because of your faith-love relationship to Him!

Had you *perfect* faith and *perfect* love, you could enjoy His *perfect* life—but these you do not have. For although you have been restored to life by the presence of the Holy Spirit within your human spirit, there is no eradication of the flesh, which (as you will see represented in the illustration on page 77 in figure D by the smaller inner circle containing the capital I) is still operative within the human soul. The wrong man still clings tenaciously to his seat at the keyboard of the grand piano and resists every attempt on the part of the right Man to take over!

This is the problem of the carnal Christian, who although indwelt by the Holy Spirit is still dominated to a large degree by the flesh. The image of the invisible God is only partially restored, as indicated in the illustration by the marginal ring around circle D, half black—representing still the works of the flesh—and half gray—representing the fruits of the Spirit. Only in certain areas of the carnal Christian's life and to a limited degree is the Lord Jesus allowed to be Himself and to express Himself through the behavior mechanism of the believer placed only spasmodically at His disposal.

In other words, though you may be redeemed and regenerate, God never deprives you of your moral capacity to choose. The act of changing your mind about Adam's change of mind, which constituted your conversion and brought about your reconciliation to God through faith in Christ, must be followed by an attitude that perpetuates the change of mind if you are to enter experientially into all the good of the new life in Christ, of whose divine nature you have become a partaker (see 2 Pet. 1:4).

If the initial act of faith was genuine by which you were redeemed (and you will only be redeemed if the initial act of faith was genuine), your subsequent attitude will never change the consequences of the act. You will remain redeemed by His "one sacrifice for sins for ever" (Heb. 10:12, KJV) and irrevocably "sealed with the promised Holy Spirit" (Eph. 1:13) by whom God "[has also appropriated and acknowledged us as His by] putting His seal upon us and giving us His [Holy] Spirit in our hearts as the security deposit and guarantee [of the fulfillment of His promise]" (2 Cor. 1:22, AMP). But your subsequent attitude will determine, on your way to heaven, how far it will be possible for the Lord Jesus Christ to implement in you that for which He has redeemed you!

It is your inherent right to choose that enables you to enter into this unique relationship with Christ—or to reject Him. But you reject Him at your peril! It has been magnificently demonstrated in the film *City of the Bees*, produced by Moody Bible Institute, that there is an instinctive interlock between this tiny insect and its behavior patterns, as in the case of every other form of animal life, only man excepted. Upon the efficiency of this interlock its very existence and survival depend. Remove the interlock, and order would be swallowed up in chaos. The social, logistic, structural and administrative problems of a bee society would be way and beyond the mental capacity of the most progressive individual bee! Anarchy would inevitably precede disaster and extinction.

No such interlock exists between man and his behavior patterns, for God created man to be a moral being, to enter into all the hidden depths of this amazing mystery—the mystery of godliness. The only interlock, the interlock of faith and love to God, allows Him to reproduce Himself in man and to make man man after the immaculate image of his Maker!

Remove this interlock, and little wonder that across the rubble of a wrecked society of men, a lonely cross has cast its shadow—the shadow of a lonely God waiting for men to be made men again as God intended men to be. And it takes God to be a man!

That is why it takes Christ to be a Christian—for Christ in a Christian puts God back into the man.

10

How Much Are You Worth?

He died for all, that those who live might no longer live for themselves but for him who for their sake died and was raised.
2 Corinthians 5:15

*C*hrist died to kill death dead and to swallow it up in victory! He drew its sting—for "the sting of death is sin" (1 Cor. 15:56), and He "appeared once for all at the end of the ages to put away sin by the sacrifice of himself" (Heb. 9:26). This He did for all men without exception, "not willing that any should perish, but that all should come to repentance" (2 Pet. 3:9, KJV).

Never allow anyone to deceive you into believing that God has placed an arbitrary limitation upon the efficacy of the blood of Christ or that there are those who cannot repent, even if they would, simply because God has deliberately placed them outside the scope of His redemptive purpose! This blasphemes the grace, love and integrity of God and makes Him morally responsible for the unbelief of the unbeliever, for the impenitence of the impenitent. It saddles Him squarely with the guilt of the guilty—as an aider and abettor of their sin!

Such is not the teaching of the Bible, for the Lord Jesus Christ made it abundantly clear that the reluctance is on man's part, not on God's: "O Jerusalem, Jerusalem, the city that kills the prophets and stones those who are sent to it! How often would I have gathered your children together as a hen gathers her brood under her wings, and you were not willing!" (Luke 13:34).

It is equally clear from the Savior's lips that the wrath of God abides on those who do not believe and that these will not see life, for "this is the judgment: the light has come into the world, and people loved the darkness rather than the light because their works were evil" (John 3:19). Whether men love light or love darkness, God or the devil, heaven or hell, love can only be expressed by the exercise of a free will. Without freedom of choice it is equally impossible to obey or to disobey—to be commended for the one or to be condemned for the other!

I cannot blame my typewriter for the spelling mistakes it makes nor congratulate it for its beautiful prose—it is an impersonal machine. It neither offers its services nor withholds them, for it has no capacity to choose. Yet it is precisely at this point that men are held morally responsible to God, who will take vengeance "on those who do not know God and on those who do not obey the gospel of our Lord Jesus. They will suffer the punishment of eternal destruction, away from the presence of the Lord and from the glory of his might" (2 Thess. 1:8–9).

Some would have you believe that only those can obey the gospel and accept Christ as their Savior to whom God has given the ability to obey as a purely arbitrary, mechanical act on His part, leaving no option in the matter to any individual either way. On the basis of this strange hypothesis, the fearful judgment of God is to fall upon those who have remained in their rebellious state of unbelief only because they have been unable to exercise an ability to obey the gospel that only God can give—and that He has refused to give them! Needless to say, such an idea can only serve to bring the righteousness and judgment of God into contempt and disrepute.

The revelation that God has given to us by His Holy Spirit through the apostles is delightfully clear: "If anyone does sin, we have an advocate with the Father, Jesus Christ the righteous. He is the propitiation for our sins, and not for ours only but also for the sins of the whole world" (1 John 2:1–2). He "gave himself as a ransom for all" (1 Tim. 2:6) "so that by the grace of God he might taste death for everyone" (Heb. 2:9).

It is your inherent right to choose, which is at the very heart of the mystery—both the mystery of godliness and the mystery of iniquity. For as we began to see in the fourth chapter, it is man's ability to say yes to God in a faith-love relationship of total dependence, producing godliness, that gives him alternatively the ability to say no to God in independence—to become a soul dominated by the flesh and producing iniquity.

The cross involves for all men everywhere a personal decision that cannot be avoided. For God now "commands all people everywhere to repent, because he has fixed a day on which he will judge the world in righteousness by a man whom he has appointed; and of this he has given assurance to all by raising him from the dead" (Acts 17:30–31).

This is the compelling love of Christ. God's command to all men everywhere to repent is an invitation to life! He does not mock men who are sorry for their sin, nor does He command men to repent of their sin who cannot be sorry.

"The love of Christ controls us, because we have concluded this: that one has died for all, therefore all have died" (2 Cor. 5:14). The fact that the Lord Jesus Christ died for all is ample corroboration of the fact that "in Adam" all died. Men are spiritually dead, "alienated from the life of God" (Eph. 4:18)— their lamps are out! How thrilling and wonderful to know, however, that "as in Adam all die, so also in Christ shall all be made alive" (1 Cor. 15:22).

You can know the indwelling presence of the risen Lord resident within your human spirit by His Holy Spirit from the very moment that you receive Christ as your Redeemer. You are then no longer waiting for the resurrection—you are enjoying it!

It is true, of course, that there will be a physical resurrection of the body, for "this perishable nature must clothe itself with what is imperishable, and this mortality must clothe itself with immortality" (15:53, WEY). But this is only incidental compared with the priceless privilege of sharing now the very life of the Lord Jesus Christ Himself!

Consider further with me, however, this important passage in Second Corinthians 5:15: "He died for all, so that all those who live might live no longer to and for themselves, but to and for Him Who died and was raised again for their sake" (AMP). When the apostle refers to "all those who live," he is speaking of those who have already been raised from the dead spiritually. They are no longer "in Adam"—dead—they are "in Christ"—alive! He goes on to explain to what end God has raised them to life again. It is that they may no longer live "to and for themselves" but "to and for Him Who died and was raised again for their sake."

In other words, there is to be a remarkable change of attitude and outlook, for Christ died and rose again from the dead to introduce an entirely new principle of human behavior. To live "to and for yourself" is to "walk after the flesh." To live "to and for Christ" is to "walk after the Spirit"!

These are the two principles of human behavior. It is not just a matter of degree, it is a matter of kind: to be dominated by the flesh is to be dominated by the devil, and to be dominated by the Spirit is to be dominated by God. Two men doing identically the same thing may at the same time, by their identical act, be demonstrating two different principles of behavior that are diametrically opposed to each other.

Both Cain and Abel brought an offering to the Lord (see Gen. 4:3–8), and to the undiscerning, it would appear that both were engaged in a sincere act of worship. Yet Cain and his offering were both rejected, and God had no regard for them.

Was it the act that God rejected and that made Cain unacceptable? No, it was the principle that governed the act—a principle that made the otherwise innocent act as sinful as the principle that prompted it. He was still living "to and for himself."

Sin was still lying at the door—the flesh was still dominant. Cain was still convinced of his own superior judgment as to what was good for him, and for that matter, as to what was good for God! He "brought to the Lord an offering of the fruit of the ground" (4:3)—the ground that God had cursed (see 3:17). Cain "was of the evil one [the devil] and murdered his brother. And why did he murder him? Because"—*in the very act of "worship"*—"his own deeds were evil and his brother's righteous" (1 John 3:12).

To bring an offering to the Lord was for Cain just another way of letting "the evil one" give expression to his undying hatred of God and to his unremitting hostility to the Son, for the offering that he brought was in deliberate defiance of the spiritual significance of the lamb that Abel offered. An act of "worship" ended up in an act of cold-blooded murder. But though there may have been some difference in degree between the acts, there was absolutely no difference in kind. It was the devil himself and no other—who, as we have already seen, "was a murderer from the beginning" (John 8:44)—who inspired both the act of "worship" and the act of killing Abel. There was death in Cain's religion! When God called his bluff, he was furious and exposed himself for the devil's dupe he was.

It would not really matter whether as a professor in a theological seminary you denied the virgin birth of Christ, as a pastor from the pulpit you discredited the atoning efficacy of the blood He shed or as a church member you participated in those apostate forms of Christless "Christianity" that repudiate His deity and His sinlessness, or drove the nails into His hands and feet upon the cross. All would be equally satisfying to the devil!

Abel, on the other hand, through faith "offered to God a more acceptable sacrifice than Cain did, and through this faith he obtained testimony that he was righteous, God giving the testimony by accepting his gifts" (Heb. 11:4, WEY). It was certainly not the monetary value of the lamb that made either Abel or his gift acceptable, for it may well have been far less than the value of the offering that Cain had brought.

Wherein, then, lay Abel's acceptability? It was in the principle that governed his act, a principle that demanded total obedience to God out of an attitude of total dependence.

By faith Abel appropriated the spiritual significance of the little lamb as the symbol of the Lamb of God who takes away the sin of the world. In humble anticipation he sheltered beneath the "faith shadow" of a future cross upon which the Prince of Peace would die to kill death dead and to bring him, Abel, back to life again! "The Lord had regard for Abel and his offering" (Gen. 4:4).

What is the principle that governs your behavior? I am not asking you the nature of your behavior—I am asking you the principle from which it springs!

You will remember that we have seen sin defined in the Bible as independence: "Whatever does not proceed from faith is sin" (Rom. 14:23). It is an attitude of "lawlessness" (1 John 3:4). What then does repentance involve? It involves stepping out of independence back into dependence—and the measure of your repentance will be the measure of your dependence!

Every area of your life in which you have not learned to be dependent is an area of your life in which you have not as yet repented. Perhaps you are a businessman, and you imagine that once you have crossed the threshold of your office—you are the boss! Everything you say goes! This is your little kingdom—perhaps even a mighty empire—and you congratulate yourself upon the fact that you have just what it takes to outbid your competitor or to outsmart your opponents. You need Christ for your Sunday school class, and you need Christ for some of the other church responsibilities that you shoulder, but right there in the city amidst the stern demands of modern commerce, you are out on your own. It is sink or swim by the might of your own right arm.

Sir! That is just the area in your life in which you have *not yet repented!*

Maybe you are a mother, and if there is one thing for which you consider yourself to be completely adequate, it is the business of rearing a family! What you have not learned about child psychology is hardly worth knowing, and the discipline of a well-planned family life leaves you little opportunity to get upon your knees. Bathwater and baby powder have stronger claims upon your time than prayer, and pride of house takes precedence over humility of heart.

Madam! This is just the area of your life in which you have *not yet repented!*

The words flow like water running down a mountain stream when you stand up in the pulpit and intoxicate your congregation with your latest verbal masterpiece. The logic is supreme and the anecdotes are apt, while a dignified deportment gives added point to weighty utterances already underlined by gentle gestures with the hands. Aunt Agatha was right when she said that you would one day be a preacher—but she did not know how fine a preacher you would be! You have all that it takes to build a thriving church.

Preacher! The pulpit is the place! The place in which you have *not yet repented!*

Is it your beautiful voice or your musical talent? Is it your athletic skill or your academic gift? In what part of your life are you adequate without Christ—in which to lose Him would be to lose nothing? That is it! Right there! That is the place in your life in which you have *not yet repented!*

You have been "made alive" (Col. 2:13) in Christ to be exclusively at His disposal so that by the Holy Spirit He may monopolize your total personality and give expression to Himself through you in your behavior. This is what it means to be "filled with the Spirit" (Eph. 5:18), or to be "godly," as represented by figure E in the diagram. The capital I is on the cross, and as indicated by the gray margin at the circumference of circle E, all that you do is what Christ does and creates in you the image of all that Christ is! "I have been crucified with Christ, and it is no longer I that live, but Christ that lives in me; and the life which I now live in the body I live through faith in the Son of God who loved me and gave Himself up to death on my behalf" (Gal. 2:20, WEY).

The image will never be perfect or complete down here on earth, but the degree in which by your free consent you live to and for Christ is the degree of your spirituality. The degree in which you still live to and for yourself is the degree of your carnality—and the degree in which you have not as yet repented!

It may be, however, that up till now your experience as a Christian has been one of consistent defeat. You are baffled and bewildered at your own impotence and almost in despair of any possibility of improvement. Sometimes you cry from your heart,

> I find therefore the law of my nature to be that when I desire to do what is right, evil is lying in ambush for me. For in my inmost self all my sympathy is with the Law of God; but I discover within me a different Law at war with the Law of my understanding, and leading me captive to the Law which is everywhere at work in my body—the Law of sin. (Unhappy man that I am! who will rescue me from this death-burdened body?) (Rom. 7:21–24, WEY)

There is war in your soul, and you will always be baffled and perplexed until you recognize what I have constantly reiterated: that within the soul of every regenerate person there are two powerful forces at work: the constant down-drag of the old Adamic nature and the mighty liberating power of Christ the Lord. "To sum up then, with my understanding, I—my true self—am in servitude to the Law of God, but with my lower nature I am in servitude to the Law of sin" (Rom. 7:25, WEY).

There are two appetites at work within you: one insatiably hungry for all that is evil and hostile to God and the other insatiably hungry for all that is pure and noble, wholesome and true. The one has its origin in the devil, the other in God. To be in ignorance of this fact or to act in defiance of it will make you as foolish as the Galatian Christians, to whom the apostle Paul put the following question: "Are you so foolish and so senseless and so silly? Having begun [your new life spiritually] with the [Holy] Spirit, are you now reaching perfection [by dependence] on the flesh?" (Gal. 3:3, AMP). Having received the very life of Christ through the Spirit, the only source of godliness, these foolish Galatians then tried to live the Christian life in the energy of the flesh, which is only the source of iniquity. They tried to make the leopard change its spots!

Is this what you have been doing? Having received everything that God can give you in Christ, have you been living as though God has given you nothing—as though everything depended on you?

It is as though you were born with a battered, old-vintage Ford car in the garage, one that has broken springs, faulty brakes and dirty plugs—the flesh! Then you are born again, and there is a brand-new Cadillac—the Spirit—alongside the rusty old Ford in the garage. But instead of going out in the brand-new Cadillac, you drive around in your old tin crate—honking, snorting, puffing and blowing in a cloud of smoke, "giving your testimony" and telling folk about your lovely new car!

Your testimony would be as flat as your tires! You would spend all your time asking God for spares: "O God, please give me new springs; and please God, give me new plugs!" and God would do nothing of the sort. He would say, "Stick it in the dump! It's only fit for the scrap heap—so bury it! Go out in the brand-new Cadillac I have given you—it has power enough and to spare!" For "it is the Spirit who gives life; the flesh is no help at all" (John 6:63).

The death of Christ upon the cross accomplished something much more than your redemption from the penalty of sin. It put your pride on the scrapheap and you in the dump!

However little we may be able to explain it, "we know that our old (unrenewed) self was nailed to the cross with Him in order that [our] body [which is the instrument] of sin might be made ineffective and inactive for evil, that we might no longer be the slaves of sin" (Rom. 6:6, AMP).

In other words, as shown in the illustration on page 77 by the center circle in figure E, there must not only be a cross on the hill but a cross in your heart!

The self that sin makes of you was taken by the Lord Jesus Christ into death with Him—that you might be delivered not only from sin's penalty but also from its power. Your soul is released from sin's evil influence so that you may become the self that Christ makes of you: "a new creation. The old has passed away; behold, the new has come" (2 Cor. 5:17).

The capital I has been crucified with Christ so that God may have right-of-way into every area of your personality, at liberty to reproduce Himself once more in you and transform you into His own likeness. And that is godliness!

> We were buried therefore with Him by the baptism into death, so that just as Christ was raised from the dead by the glorious [power] of the Father, so we too might [habitually] live and behave in newness of life. For if we have become one with Him by sharing a death like His, we shall also be [one with Him in sharing] His resurrection [by a new life lived for God]. (Rom. 6:4–5, AMP)

However, just as the death of Christ for you is only potential until by a deliberate and voluntary act of faith you appropriate its efficacy for your redemption, so your death with Christ is only potential unless by a deliberate and voluntary attitude of faith you appropriate its efficacy for your sanctification—enabling God to put you once more to that intelligent use for which He created you and for which Christ has now redeemed you:

> By the death He died, He died to sin [ending His relation to it] once for all; and the life that He lives, He is living to God [in unbroken fellowship with Him]. Even so consider yourselves also dead to sin and your relation to it broken, but alive to God [living in unbroken fellowship with Him] in Christ Jesus. (6:10–11, AMP)

You are to live exclusively "to and for Christ" by virtue of what you are in Him. You cannot accomplish your own redemption, and you cannot accomplish your own sanctification. It is "His divine power [that] has granted to us all things that pertain to life and godliness, through the knowledge of him who called us to his own glory and excellence" (2 Pet. 1:3). *Faith takes* what *God gives*, and *God gives* what *man needs! All* that he needs!

All that God gives, which is all that you need, He gives to you in Christ, "that no human being might boast in the presence of God. And because of him you are in Christ Jesus, who became to us wisdom from God, righteousness and sanctification and redemption" (1 Cor. 1:29–30).

The degree to which by a deliberate, voluntary attitude of faith you are reckoning yourself to be dead with Christ to all that you are in Adam and alive to God in all that you are in Christ is the degree to which the redemptive purpose of God has been wrought out in your life—and this is the only valid estimate of your worth! Everything else is a dead loss. "Consequently, from now on we estimate and regard no one from a [purely] human point of view [in terms of natural standards of value]" (2 Cor. 5:16, AMP).

Pointing to an affluent-looking gentleman coming into the church, I might say to you (if I were mischievous enough), "How much is he worth?" and maybe you would reply, "If he's worth a dollar, he's worth a million!" And I would say to you, "I did not ask *how much money he had in the bank!* I simply asked you how much he was *worth!*"

A man could have all the money in all the banks in all the world and be worth nothing—so far as God is concerned—if he were still living "to and for himself." The measure of a man's worth is the measure in which he no longer lives "to and for himself" but "to and for Jesus Christ." *No more and no less!*

How much are *you* worth?

You tell me that you have just completed your church building program, and that the board has just appointed a new minister. That's fine, but pardon me for asking—how much is the minister worth? "Why," you say, "he has a most distinguished academic record," and you begin to enlarge upon the letters after his name. But you will forgive me if I interrupt, I am sure. It is excellent that a man should take the trouble to be highly qualified, but I did not ask you how clever he was at mastering facts or in passing examinations, I simply asked how much he was worth!

A man's worth is not primarily a matter of scholarship, it is essentially a matter of relationship—relationship to Jesus Christ. It is, of course, perfectly possible and perfectly legitimate to have both, and this is to be commended. But we should always remind ourselves,

> That which the world deems foolish in God is wiser than men's wisdom, and that which it deems feeble in God is mightier than men's might. For consider, brethren, God's call to you. Not many who are wise with merely human wisdom, not many of position and influence, not many of noble birth have been called. But God has chosen the things which the world regards as foolish, in order to put its wise men to shame; and God has chosen the things which the world regards as destitute of influence, in order to put its powerful things to shame; and the things which the world regards as base, and those things which it sets utterly at naught—things that have no existence—God has chosen in order to reduce to nothing things that do exist; to prevent any mortal man from boasting in the presence of God. (1 Cor. 1:25–29, WEY)

How much are you worth?

There was a time when Paul the apostle, as Saul of Tarsus, hated Christ and persecuted the church. He had done so because he had still regarded Christ from a purely human point of view—in terms of natural standards of value. Had these natural standards of value been spiritually valid, Saul of Tarsus would have been right, and Paul the apostle would have been wrong!

To Saul, according to all the facts as he knew them and as they were commonly accepted by all the people who "mattered," Jesus Christ was the illegitimate child of an unfaithful woman. So by all normally accepted standards of society, He was an outcast! Socially how much was Christ worth? Nothing!

Born of peasant stock, His schooling was negligible, sufficing only to equip Him for the humble duties of a common craftsman. Professionally how much was He worth? Nothing!

A fanatical street preacher and a rabble rouser, He was totally repudiated by all the ecclesiastical dignitaries of His day, and having had absolutely no theological training whatever, was looked upon with supreme contempt by all that called itself scholarship among those who searched the Scriptures. Ecclesiastically, theologically and intellectually how much was He worth? Nothing!

His financial standing was such that He even had to borrow a coin for one of His farfetched illustrations! He was an incorrigible scrounger by all natural standards of value, for He had no home of His own. Born in a borrowed stable, He lived and dined in borrowed homes; He rode upon a borrowed donkey, was crucified on a borrowed cross and buried in a borrowed tomb! He was bankrupt from the start. Financially how much was He worth? By all natural standards of value—nothing!

Shall we be angry with Saul of Tarsus? Was his judgment insincere? Were the conclusions to which he came not entirely reasonable? If the Lord Jesus Christ were to appear in the world today under similar circumstances, what congregation would call Him to be its pastor? What university or Bible college or training institute would appoint Him to its faculty?

What missionary organization would invite Him on its board or even send Him to the field? Who would make Him chairman of the building committee?

Maybe our standards of value are as wrong today as were those of Saul in his day!

Something happened, however, that changed Saul of Tarsus completely. His old standards of value went by the board, and everything assumed an entirely new perspective!

The values themselves had not changed—it was simply that in a dazzling encounter on the road to Damascus, Saul of Tarsus saw "the glory of God in the face of Jesus Christ" (2 Cor. 4:6). He looked into the face of a man and saw God, and he was blinded by the sight, for he saw "the perfect imprint and very image of [God's] nature" (Heb. 1:3, AMP).

In one blinding, crushing moment of humiliation, his own utter worthlessness was exposed to the stubborn heart of this proud enemy of the faith! "Circumcised on the eighth day, of the people of Israel, of the tribe of Benjamin, a Hebrew of Hebrews; as to the law, a Pharisee; as to zeal, a persecutor of the church; as to righteousness under the law, blameless" (Phil. 3:5–6), by all natural standards of value this man was worth everything—and had already outstripped many of his Jewish contemporaries in his boundless devotion to the traditions of his ancestors (see Gal. 1:14). But in the light of this new discovery of God, he could only say,

> Every advantage that I had gained I considered lost for Christ's sake. Yes, and I look upon everything as loss compared with the overwhelming gain of knowing Jesus Christ my Lord. For his sake I did in actual fact suffer the loss of everything, but I considered it useless rubbish compared with being able to win Christ. For now my

place is in him, and I am not dependent upon any of the self-achieved righteousness of the Law. God has given me that genuine righteousness which comes from faith in Christ. (Phil. 3:7–9, Phillips)

Saul of Tarsus suddenly discovered that a man is worth only as much as can be seen of God in him. He realized that he was in the presence of the man in whom (to use his own description) "the whole fullness of Deity (the Godhead) continues to dwell in bodily form [giving complete expression of the divine nature]" (Col. 2:9, AMP) and that this man was Jesus Christ, whom he was persecuting! From that moment on, nothing else mattered.

Saul of Tarsus stopped being Saul of Tarsus and became Paul the apostle. He was out of Adam, and he was in Christ, and the "law of the Spirit of life" began to operate, introducing the new principle of human behavior that made him a "new creature."

Paul had found reality in God, and the show was over! He could afford to discard his "makeup" and lay aside the musty costumes of a religious performance. The pompous self-esteem of a godless society no longer impressed him, nor did the honors it could bestow upon its servile devotees.

The apostle was emancipated! He was released from the hollow art of living in a fool's paradise of faulty values—a world of artificial standards anchored to a cloud and blown by every wind of fashion. "God forbid," he says, "that I should glory, save in the cross of our Lord Jesus Christ, by whom the world is crucified unto me, and I unto the world" (Gal. 6:14, KJV)!

Losing his life, he found it! Dying to self and buried with Christ, he found himself alive again—in God. For in that blinding flash of glory on the Damascus road, the whole mystery of godliness became an open secret in the face of Jesus Christ!

He had discovered how much he was worth: nothing! To discover that is to discover how much Christ is worth: everything!

When you are willing to obey what you have discovered and to let the truth behave, then the Lord Jesus Christ will fill what you are—nothing—with what He is—everything—and that indeed will be something!

With the wrong man out and the right Man in, how wealthy God will have made you! Good friend, before you lay this book aside, embrace by faith these great and precious promises, and commit yourself to Christ for all that which He is committed to in you. He waits to fill you with Himself and to share with you the secret of the mystery—"the mystery hidden for ages and generations but now revealed to his saints. To them God chose to make known how great among the Gentiles are the riches of the glory of this mystery, which is Christ in you, the hope of glory" (Col. 1:26–27).

Notes

Chapter 1

1. Editor's note: Statistical and cultural data in this book reflect the time and context of the book's original writing in Great Britain in 1964.

2. Editor's note: American church attendance today, as opposed to the 60 percent mentioned by W. Ian Thomas, is shown by many polls to be at around 40 percent, although actual attendance, according to some researchers, appears to be closer to 20 percent. See Rebecca Barnes and Lindy Lowry, "7 Startling Facts: An Up Close Look at Church Attendance in America," [online] ChurchLeaders, www.churchleaders.com/pastors/pastor-articles/139575-7-startling-facts-an-up-closer-look-at-church-attendance-in-america.html, accessed September 22, 2014, and "Religious Landscape Survey" [online] Pew Research Religion and Public Life Project, pewforum.org/affiliations, accessed September 22, 2014.

Chapter 5

1. T.C. Hammond, *In Understanding Be Men: An Introductory Handbook on Christian Doctrine* (Downers Grove, IL: InterVarsity Press, 1961).

PUBLICATIONS
Fort Washington, PA 19034

This book is published by CLC Publications, an outreach of CLC Ministries International. The purpose of CLC is to make evangelical Christian literature available to all nations so that people may come to faith and maturity in the Lord Jesus Christ. We hope this book has been life changing and has enriched your walk with God through the work of the Holy Spirit. If you would like to know more about CLC, we invite you to visit our website:
www.clcusa.org

To know more about the remarkable story of the founding of CLC International we encourage you to read

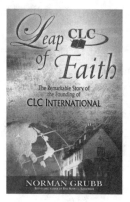

LEAP OF FAITH

Norman Grubb

Paperback
Size 5¹/₄ x 8, Pages 248
ISBN: 978-0-87508-650-7
ISBN (*e-book*): 978-1-61958-055-8

TORCHBEARERS
international

The Torchbearers of the Capernwray Missionary
Fellowship is an international Christian
organization that provides both
short-term Bible Schools and retreats in
twenty-five worldwide locations.

For more information about Torchbearers visit
www.torchbearers.org
